A* GCSE PHYSICS

THE MANCHESTER GRAMMAR SCHOOL

OXFORD
UNIVERSITY PRESS

OXFORD
UNIVERSITY PRESS

Great Clarendon Street, Oxford OX2 6DP

Oxford University Press is a department of the University of Oxford.
It furthers the University's objective of excellence in research, scholarship, and education by publishing worldwide in

Oxford New York

Athens Auckland Bangkok Bogotá Buenos Aires Calcutta
Cape Town Chennai Dar es Salaam Delhi Florence Hong Kong Istanbul
Karachi Kuala Lumpur Madrid Melbourne Mexico City Mumbai
Nairobi Paris São Paulo Singapore Taipei Tokyo Toronto Warsaw
with associated companies in Berlin Ibadan

First published 1999

British Library Cataloguing in Publication Data
Data available

ISBN 0 19 914743 4 (school edition)
0 19 914750 7 (bookshop edition)

First published by the Minute Hand Group.

The Minute Hand Group would like to thank Mr and Mrs Khvat, Dr and Mrs Shapiro, and Mr C. Mayo for their support.

Typeset by Advance Typesetting Limited, Long Hanborough, Oxon
Printed in Great Britain

preface

The idea for the book which you are now reading came from a group of pupils at The Manchester Grammar School. Their year achieved what some league tables at least reckoned were the best GCSE grades in the country, yet they had found a dearth of good revision guides aimed specifically at able students. They thought they could do better, and the result (as part of the Young Enterprise Scheme) was the best-selling *Physics A* GCSE Revision Guide – written by the students for the students*. The rest, as they say, is history … . The three Guides in this new series produced by the Oxford University Press are written by the same type of people who actually sit GCSEs – the candidates. They are wholly user-friendly, and we hope also that they are exciting in a way few other revision guides can achieve.

I hope you enjoy working with them as much as all of us here have enjoyed being involved in their production. Royalties from these books go to The Manchester Grammar School Foundation Bursary Fund, which pays for pupils whose parents have low incomes to attend the School; thank you for your help.

Martin Stephen

Dr Martin Stephen
High Master
Manchester Grammar School

contents

preface 3

topic one mechanics **6**
- *Kinematics* 6
- *Speed, velocity and acceleration* 6
- *The 'suvat' equations* 8
- *Projectiles* 10
- *Force, momentum and energy* 11
- *Energy and work* 11
- *Momentum* 14
- *More about forces* 17

topic two waves **24**
- *Describing and measuring waves* 24
- *Ripple tank pictures: reflection and refraction* 25
- *Special properties of waves: diffraction and interference* 26
- *The electromagnetic spectrum* 27
- *Sound* 29

topic three optics **33**
- *Shadows* 33
- *Reflection* 34
- *Refraction* 35
- *Total internal reflection* 37
- *Lenses* 38
- *The eye* 43

topic four electricity **46**
- *Static electricity* 46
- *Electric circuits* 46
- *Potential difference* 47
- *Series and parallel circuits* 47
- *Resistance* 48
- *Power and energy* 52
- *Mains electricity* 53

topic five electricity and magnetism **56**
- *Magnets* 56
- *Magnetic materials and making magnets* 56
- *Magnetic fields* 57
- *The magnetic effect of a current* 58
- *Motor effect* 60
- *The direct current (d.c.) motor* 61

topic six electromagnetic induction **64**
- *The dynamo or generator effect* 64
- *A simple alternating current (a.c.) generator* 66
- *Transformers* 66

topic seven electronics **70**
Important components 70
Systems 76
Digital electronics 77
topic eight nuclear physics **80**
Atomic structure 80
Radioactive decay 81
Nuclear energy 84
topic nine thermal physics **88**
The kinetic theory of matter 88
Conduction, convection and radiation 89
topic nine-and-a-half the Earth and beyond **94**
Life, the universe and everything 94
Our solar system 95
appendix a:
Laws and equations 98
appendix b:
Hints and tips 104
index **106**

topic one

mechanics

Kinematics

Speed, velocity and acceleration

Distance how far you travel irrespective of direction

Displacement how far you are from your starting point – direction as well as distance. For example a distance could be 5 metres, but the displacement may be +5 m or –5 m. If you walk 5 m forwards, then 5 m backwards, then the distance is 10 metres (5 m + 5 m) but the displacement is 0 m (5 m + –5 m)

Example question

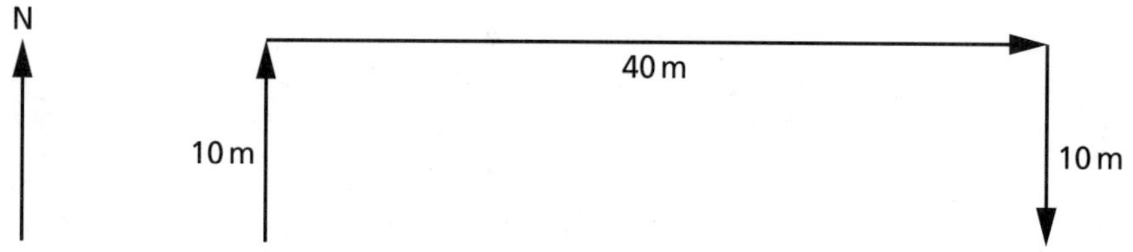

Find:

a) The total distance travelled.
b) The final displacement north, where north is positive.
c) Where east is positive, the final displacement east.

Answers:

a) The distance travelled is 10 + 40 + 10 = 60 m. This is because the question is only about the distance travelled in total, disregarding direction.
b) The displacement north is 10 – 10 = 0 m. This is because although 10 m north has been travelled, 10 m south has also been travelled. Thus the displacement is actually zero since the end point is no further north than the starting point.
c) Now taking east as the positive direction, you can disregard movement in north and south directions, as we are only interested in movement east and west. 40 m has been travelled east so the answer is 40 m.

Speed the rate of change of distance

$$\text{Average speed} = \frac{\text{distance travelled}}{\text{time taken}}$$

The unit of speed is metres per second (m/s).

Velocity how fast you travel in a specified direction, that is, the rate of change of displacement

$$\text{Average velocity} = \frac{\text{change in displacement}}{\text{time taken}}$$

$$v = \frac{s}{t}$$

v	velocity (m/s)
s	displacement (m)
t	time (s)

Acceleration the change in velocity over the time taken for the change.

$$\text{Acceleration} = \frac{\text{change in velocity}}{\text{change in time}} = \frac{\text{final velocity} - \text{initial velocity}}{\text{time taken}}$$

$$a = \frac{\Delta \text{velocity}}{\Delta \text{time}} = \frac{v-u}{t}$$

a	acceleration (m/s^2)
v	final velocity (m/s)
u	initial velocity (m/s)
t	time (s)

Δ means 'change in'

The unit of acceleration is m/s^2, as it is the change in m/s per second.

Velocity and displacement are ***vector*** *quantities, as opposed to* ***scalar*** *(speed, distance). This means they have a direction, +ve or –ve, as well as a magnitude (size) whereas a scalar quantity only has a magnitude.*

Acceleration is a vector quantity, too.

Displacement–time graphs

You will need to be able to recognise the shapes of these three graphs.

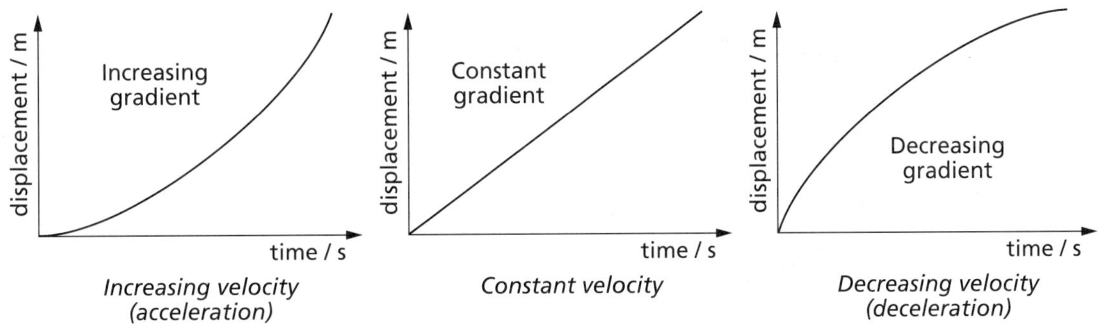

The '*suvat*' equations

At GCSE, all levels of mechanics are connected by four vital equations. These equations combine the concepts of displacement, initial velocity, final velocity, acceleration and time.

$$v = u + at$$
$$s = ut + \tfrac{1}{2}at^2$$
$$v^2 - u^2 = 2as$$
$$s = \left(\frac{u + v}{2}\right)t$$

s	displacement (m)
u	initial velocity (m/s)
v	final velocity (m/s)
a	acceleration (m/s^2)
t	time (s)

Given any three of these values, the fourth and subsequently fifth can be found, by substituting into the relevant equations, i.e. the equation containing the three known values and the required value.

These equations apply only when ***acceleration is constant*** *and* ***s, u, v and a are in the same straight line***.

Using graphs to find suvat *values*

The graph below shows velocity against time. The initial velocity, u, is shown, together with the final velocity, v. The gradient, or slope of the graph, is the acceleration. The area under the graph represents the distance travelled. Note that the line is straight, as the acceleration is constant.

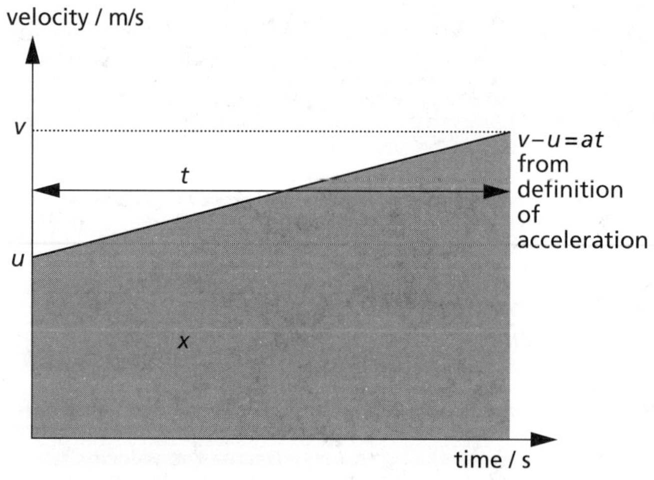

In any questions, you should use the values on the scale. Some of these will be given to you, others you will have to calculate for yourself.

Acceleration

The gradient of the line = $(v - u)/t$ = acceleration. We can rearrange the definition of acceleration:

$$a = \frac{(v - u)}{t}$$

$$\Rightarrow at = v - u$$

$$\Rightarrow v = u + at$$

$$\boldsymbol{v = u + at}$$

Distance travelled

The area under the graph is a trapezium. The area of a trapezium is the average of the two parallel sides, i.e. half the total length of the two parallel sides, multiplied by the distance between them. In the diagram, it is half of $(u+v)$, multiplied by the time (t).

So the distance travelled = $\boldsymbol{s = \frac{(u + v)}{2} \times t}$

However, the area under the graph is also the area of the rectangle, plus the area of the triangle. The area of the rectangle is u multiplied by t.

The area of the triangle is half base multiplied by height, or $\frac{1}{2}at \times t$ (see diagram). This gives the area of the triangle as $\frac{1}{2}at^2$. The area of the rectangle plus the area of the triangle is $ut + \frac{1}{2}at^2$.

$$\boldsymbol{s = ut + \tfrac{1}{2}at^2}$$

Taking time out!

This is some algebra that you don't have to do; you just need to know the final result.

$v = u + at$	
$\Rightarrow v^2 = (u + at)^2$	Square both sides
$= u^2 + 2uat + a^2t^2$	Multiply out the brackets
$= u^2 + 2a(ut + \frac{1}{2}at^2)$	Take out a 'factor' of 2*a*
as $s = ut + \frac{1}{2}at^2$	
$\boldsymbol{v^2 = u^2 + 2as}$	Substitute

If you can follow this algebra and learn how to shift around the letters in equations, you're doing well.

Projectiles

Drop a ball (vertically), and at the same time from the same height, throw another identical ball horizontally. It may seem surprising, but both the balls land at exactly the same time. This is because, in both cases, the acceleration due only to gravity (9.8 m/s^2 towards the Earth) is exactly the same. (We are assuming that air resistance is negligible; this makes life much easier.)

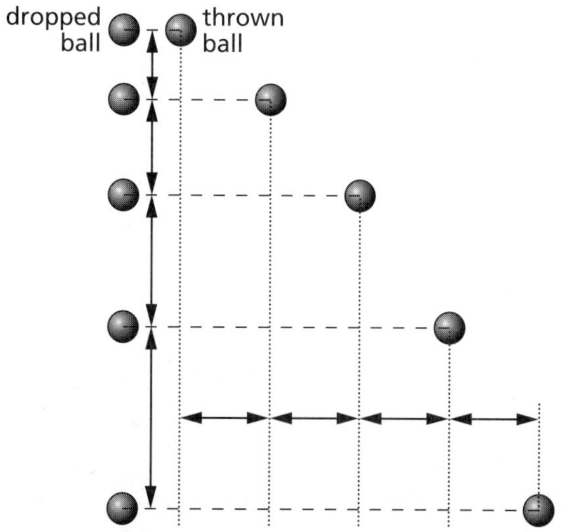

In the diagram one of the balls has been dropped and the other thrown, simultaneously. Their positions at regular intervals in time are shown.

The vertical distances between the images of the balls get bigger. This is because the balls accelerate downwards, so each time they move further. However, the ball on the right was thrown horizontally as well. You can see that the horizontal distances between the images of the ball on the right stay the same. This is because the ball on the right was travelling at a constant horizontal velocity. (Ignoring air resistance again!). However, the important thing is that both the balls are at the same vertical position each time, despite the fact that the ball on the right is moving horizontally as well. Both balls will land at the same time.

The vertical motion of a projectile is unaffected by its horizontal motion. This must be taken into account when doing calculations on projectiles.

Acceleration due to gravity on Earth = 9.8 m/s^2. Note that this is equal to the gravitational field strength (9.8 N/kg), but that the units appear different. GCSE questions will always specify what value you should use for the gravitational field strength/acceleration due to gravity (usually you are asked to use 9.8).

> *(The gravitational field strength varies, because the Earth is not exactly spherical, but don't get suicidal about it; if a figure is not given to you, 9.8 or even 10 will do. Write down which value you are using to show the examiner exactly what you are doing.)*

If an object is moving at constant speed but, at the same time, changing its direction, then its velocity is changing, so the object is accelerating. For example, although the Earth moves around the Sun at constant speed, its orbit is almost circular. So its direction is changing all the time, therefore it is actually accelerating.

Force, Momentum and Energy

Energy and work

Work the energy converted from one form to another, when a force is applied to move an object a certain distance in the direction of the force

Work is therefore related to force and distance.

The joule (J) is the SI unit of energy and work, and the newton (N) is the SI unit of force.

Where W is work, F is force, and s is the distance over which the force is applied:

Work = force × distance moved in the direction of the force

$$W = Fs$$

W	joules (J)
F	newtons (N)
s	metres (m)

Energy the capacity to do work

It comes in different forms, such as thermal, sound or heat energy. An important thing to know is the:

Principle of Conservation of Energy: *Energy can never be created or destroyed; it is converted from one form to another.*

Kinetic and gravitational potential energy

These are two important types of energy.

Kinetic energy (KE) is the energy of motion.

Gravitational potential energy (GPE) is energy that's stored on account of an object's position.

$$KE = \tfrac{1}{2}mv^2$$
$$GPE = mg\Delta h$$

KE	kinetic energy (J)
m	mass of the body (kg)
v	velocity (m/s)
GPE	gravitational potential energy (energy change because of a change in height) (J)
g	gravitational field strength (N/kg)
Δh	change in height (m) (Δ means 'change in')

Supposing a body was dropped and didn't lose any energy on the way down (for instance, in overcoming air resistance) then:
if the gravitational potential energy at the top of the fall = E
then at the bottom, the kinetic energy = E
and, in between, the kinetic energy + gravitational potential energy = E

In other words the total energy is constant at all points in the fall.
This is an example of the principle of conservation of energy.

Machines, power and efficiency

*Machines transform energy, i.e. they do **work**.*

Power the rate of doing work

$$\text{Power} = \frac{\text{energy transferred}}{\text{time}} \text{ or } \frac{\text{work done}}{\text{time taken}}$$

$$P = \frac{W}{t}$$

P power (W)
W energy (work done) (J)
t time (s)

The watt (W) is the SI unit of power.

There is energy which is useful and energy which is not, high grade and low grade. Heat (thermal energy) is low grade, because it is difficult to get any useful work from it (which has to do with something called entropy). This is why machines are not 100% efficient.

Efficiency how well a machine converts input energy into useful output energy

$$\text{Efficiency} = \frac{\text{useful energy output}}{\text{total energy input}} = \frac{\text{power output}}{\text{power input}}$$

To calculate the efficiency of a machine, multiply the answer you get from the equation above by 100 to give a percentage. Efficiency has no units.

Fuels

Fuels are chemical substances that provide usable energy as a result of changing their chemical structure. Fuels are finite or non-renewable (once they are used they can not be reused). There are however, energy resources that are renewable, these are known (unsurprisingly) as renewable energy sources. Such energy usually originates from the Sun, e.g. solar power.

Why should energy not be wasted?

- Converting energy into usable forms is a costly process.
- Burning fossil fuels releases carbon dioxide which is a major contributor to the greenhouse effect which causes global warming. Other dangerous chemicals can be released, e.g. sulphur dioxide, which causes acid rain.
- As fuels are in limited supply, and can not be renewed, eventually fuel supplies will be too low to support the population of the world.
- Burning fossil fuels wastes a lot of energy. Heat energy tends to spread out and so is not as efficient as an energy source.
- The radioactive by-products of nuclear energy production must be encased and stored for thousands of years until they decay; this is expensive and can be damaging to the environment.

Force and acceleration

Force	a push or a pull, which causes a body to change its motion, so it either accelerates or decelerates

***Newton's First Law of Motion:** If a body has no unbalanced forces acting upon it, it stays stationary, or carries on moving in a straight line, at constant speed.*

As stated above, forces cause bodies to change their motion, i.e. accelerate. How much they accelerate depends on both the force and their mass. This is a well-known form of:

***Newton's Second Law of Motion:** The acceleration of an object is proportional to the resultant force on it.*

For a constant mass

Resultant force = mass × acceleration

$\sum F = ma$

F	newtons (N)
m	kg
a	m/s^2
$\sum$	means total (in this case resultant external force, because some of the forces may be acting in opposite directions)

Weight

Weight	a measure of how much gravity pulls on an object; it is a force. It is related to the mass (m) of the object (*so note that the weight is NOT the mass*) and to the strength of the gravitational field (g)

$W = mg$

W	newtons (N)
m	kilograms (kg)
g	newtons per kilogram (N/kg)

Inertia

Inertia is the reluctance of an object to start or stop moving or change its direction. If you are travelling in a car, and suddenly you brake, you continue moving at constant velocity and hit the windscreen which is stopping. This is your reluctance to stop moving. (It might be said that your tendency to stay at rest when you wake up in the morning, unless acted upon by an external force, is an example of inertia – possibly!) Why is it easier to pull a bus single-handedly once you've got it moving? Some would say 'because you've got some momentum'. They're wrong. It's because you have overcome the inertia. Mass is a measure of a body's inertia.

Circular motion

A ball is swinging round, on the end of a piece of string. The ball is accelerating. Even though it is moving at constant speed, its velocity is constantly changing, because its direction is constantly changing. Using vectors it can be shown that the direction of the force acting on the ball is always towards the centre. Therefore it is a **centripetal** force. (And definitely not a centrifugal one!)

Momentum

Momentum the mass of an object (m) multiplied by its velocity (v); it is given the symbol p

Momentum = mass × velocity

$$p = mv$$

p	kilogram metres per second (kg m/s)
m	kg
v	m/s

Newton's Second Law can be stated as:

The force on a body is proportional to the rate of change of its momentum which takes place in the direction of the force so that:

Force applied = rate of change of momentum

$$\text{Force applied} = \frac{\text{final momentum} - \text{initial momentum}}{\text{time taken}}$$

$$F = \frac{mv - mu}{t}$$

F	force (N)
mv	final momentum (kg m/s)
mu	initial momentum (kg m/s)
t	time (s)

Rearranging:

$Ft = mv - mu$ (multiplying both sides by t)
Force × time = final momentum – initial momentum

The quantity Ft is called **impulse**, and it is measured in N s (newton seconds).

Conservation of momentum

Principle of Conservation of Momentum: *When two or more objects interact with each other, their total momentum remains unchanged provided no external resultant force is acting on them.*

Collisions and explosions

Momentum is often used when describing collisions.

Total momentum before collision = total momentum after collision
(provided no external forces are acting)

This is one example of the principle of conservation of momentum.

Remember that a collision is essentially the same as an explosion, so the principle is still true. The only difference is that the bodies are moving outwards instead of towards each other. Momentum is still conserved.

Kinetic energy, however, is not necessarily conserved in collisions although the total energy is.

The cyclist below crashes into the (stationary) wheely-bin. The bin and the cycle stick together and move along. What is the velocity of the cyclist and the bin immediately after collision? (We will assume that the wheely-bin is frictionless.)

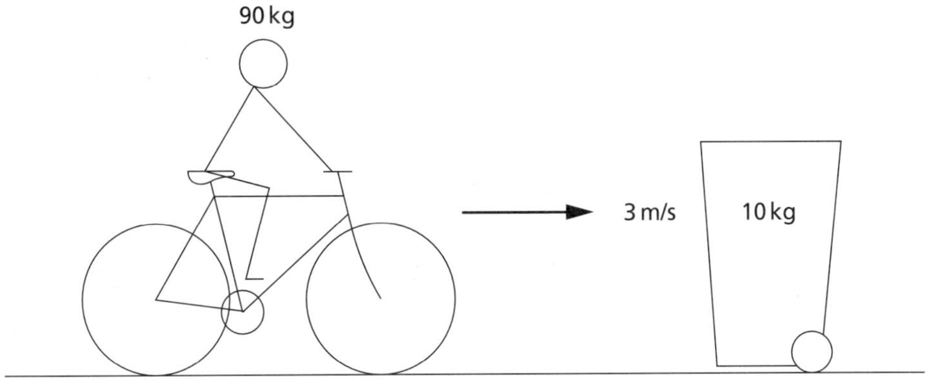

$p = mv$

So, momentum before the collision = $(90 \times 3) + (0 \times 10)$ kg m/s

= 270 kg m/s

Total momentum before collision = total momentum after collision

So the total momentum after the collision is 270 kg m/s.

The combined mass of the bike and the bin is 90 + 10 = 100 kg.

So the velocity of the bike and bin = $\frac{p}{m} = \frac{270}{100}$ = 2.7 m/s.

The total kinetic energy ($\frac{1}{2}mv^2$) before the collision is:

$(\frac{1}{2} \times 90 \times 3^2) + (\frac{1}{2} \times 10 \times 0^2)$ J

= 405 J.

However, the total kinetic energy after the collision is:

$\frac{1}{2} \times 100 \times 2.7^2$ J

= 365 J.

Not all the energy has been converted into the kinetic energy of the bike plus the bin; some has gone into doing work on the bodies (crushing the spokes, for example). Some energy is lost as thermal energy and a very little as sound. Thus the kinetic energy decreases; it is not conserved.

Collisions where kinetic energy is not conserved are called **inelastic** collisions.

An elastic collision

Take two hard balls (like snooker balls). One is moving towards the other at 4 m/s.

Before collision:

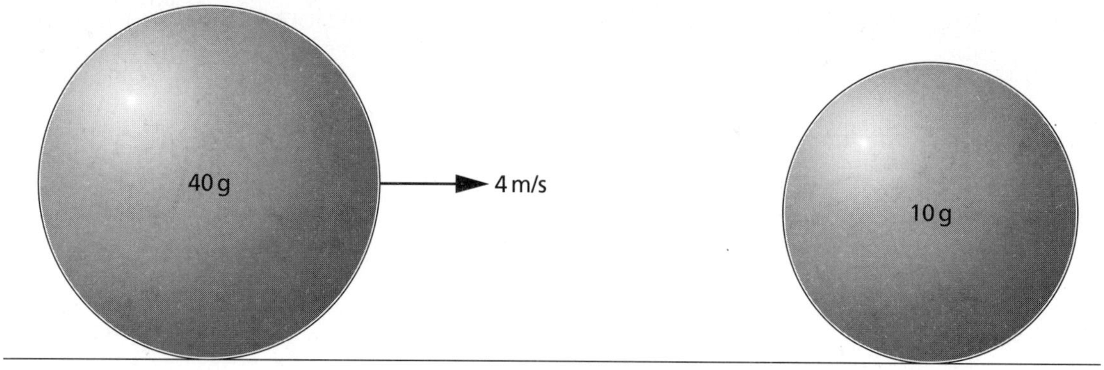

After collision:

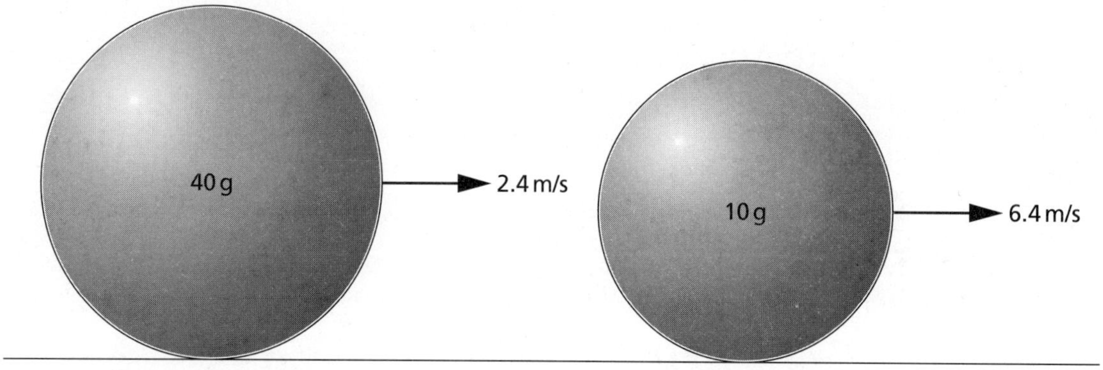

The total momentum before the collision:

$(0.04 \times 4) + 0$ kg m/s

$= 0.16$ kg m/s

The momentum after the collision is:

$(0.04 \times 2.4) + (0.01 \times 6.4)$ kg m/s

$= 0.16$ kg m/s.

The kinetic energy ($\frac{1}{2}mv^2$) before collision is:

$(\frac{1}{2} \times 0.04 \times 4^2) + (\frac{1}{2} \times 0.01 \times 0^2)$ J

$= 0.32$ J

The kinetic energy after collision is:

$(\frac{1}{2} \times 0.04 \times 2.4^2) + (\frac{1}{2} \times 0.01 \times 6.4^2)$ J

$= 0.1152 + 0.2048$ J

$= 0.32$ J

In this special case, all the kinetic energy before the collision is transformed to the kinetic energy of the balls after the collision. This is called an **elastic** collision. Other examples include a bouncy ball hitting a wall, and two boats hitting each other.

> *(Try to set out your answers neatly as shown in the example. State the equation you intend to use for your calculation before putting in the actual numbers. Line up equals signs down the page. Try not to put too many equals signs in a row horizontally. Always use words to describe what you have actually calculated.)*

More about forces

Moments

Imagine you have someone sitting on a seesaw. Their side of the seesaw moves down. It rotates around the pivot in the middle. But someone of less mass (i.e. less weight, therefore less force) can still balance the seesaw by sitting further away from the pivot. This suggests that the turning effect of a force (called its moment) is related to the force, and the distance from the pivot. And what a surprise, so it is!

Moment = force × perpendicular distance from pivot

Moment = Fd	F	newtons (N)
	d	metres (m)

Moments are therefore measured in N m, or newton metres.

> *(Although the unit for energy, the joule, is also the newton metre, the concepts of the moment of a force and of energy are completely different. With moments the distance is perpendicular to the force. So we don't use the joule as a unit for moments.)*

When a body has no unbalanced moments or forces acting on it, it is said to be in **equilibrium**.

If two bodies are in equilibrium (e.g. when the seesaw is balanced), then:

Total force acting upwards = total force acting downwards
Total force acting left = total force acting right
Total clockwise moment = total anticlockwise moment about any point.

For a worked example, see the end of topic questions.

Stability and equilibrium

Centre of gravity this is the single point where the entire weight of a body seems to act

For a body to be stable, it is best to have a centre of gravity that is low, and a base that is wide, so that, if the body is tipped, the centre of gravity will not be over a point that is outside the base.

Types of equilibrium

Stable a cone standing on its base; when you disturb it the centre of gravity rises, and the cone returns to its original position when released

Unstable an upside-down cone; the centre of gravity will fall and the cone will fall over

Neutral a cone on its side; when you disturb it the centre of gravity stays at the same height and the cone just rolls along

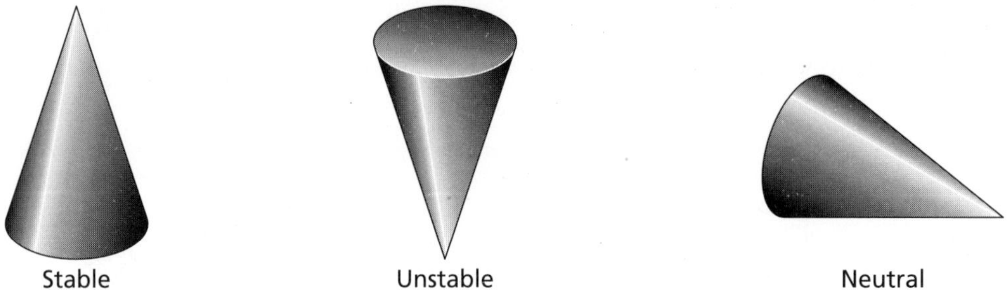

(There is also 'metastable' equilibrium, but you must wait until A-level to be enlightened about its wondrous implications for life as we know it.)

You may see the term **centre of mass**. At GCSE, your calculations involve situations where the gravitational field strength is constant, so the centre of mass is in the same position as the centre of gravity. So you don't need to worry about it.

Action and reaction

Newton's Third Law: *Every action force has an equal and opposite reaction force.*

Force and extension

If you have a spring, and you pull it, then let go, guess what happens? It springs back. (Not a pun. Well, not deliberately.) However, if you pull it too hard, it doesn't spring back to its original position. Up to that point (called the **elastic limit**), the increase in length of the spring is related to how hard you pull it: if the force is doubled, the extension is doubled.

Hooke's Law: *The extension of a spring is proportional to the stretching force (up to the elastic limit).*

Friction

Remember that friction is a force.

Nails and screws are held in by friction.

Pressure, density and Archimedes' principle

Pressure a measure of the distribution of force over an area

$$\text{Pressure} = \frac{\text{force acting normally on a surface}}{\text{area of the surface}}$$

$$P = \frac{F}{A}$$

P pressure (N/m^2), which is the same as pascals (Pa)
F force (N)
A area (m^2)

Atmospheric pressure = 101 000 Pa = 1 atmosphere. In a mercury barometer, the mercury would be at a height of 760 mm, so you may see 1 atmosphere referred to as 760 mmHg.

(Useful tip: avoid the common error of incorrect unit conversion. Be careful with:

1 m² = 10 000 cm² = 1 000 000 mm²

1 m³ = 1 000 000 cm³ = 1 000 000 000 mm³

This is easier to remember if you consider what you are actually doing, i.e.

1 m² = 100 cm × 100 cm = 10 000 cm², and not *100 cm².)*

Density this is the mass per unit volume of a substance, and it is given the symbol ρ (rho, pronounced 'roe')

$$\rho = \frac{m}{V}$$

ρ density (kg/m^3)
m mass (kg)
V volume (m^3)

Pressure in a fluid

In a fluid, pressure acts in all directions. The pressure at any point in a fluid is:

$$P = h\rho g$$

P pressure (Pa)
h depth (m)
ρ density of the fluid (kg/m^3)
g gravitational field strength (N/kg)

Archimedes' Principle: *If a body is immersed in a fluid, it experiences an upthrust force equal to the weight of fluid displaced.*

Hope you enjoyed memorising the above principle. It's not in the syllabus but it might be useful in life … if you build ships.

Worked Questions

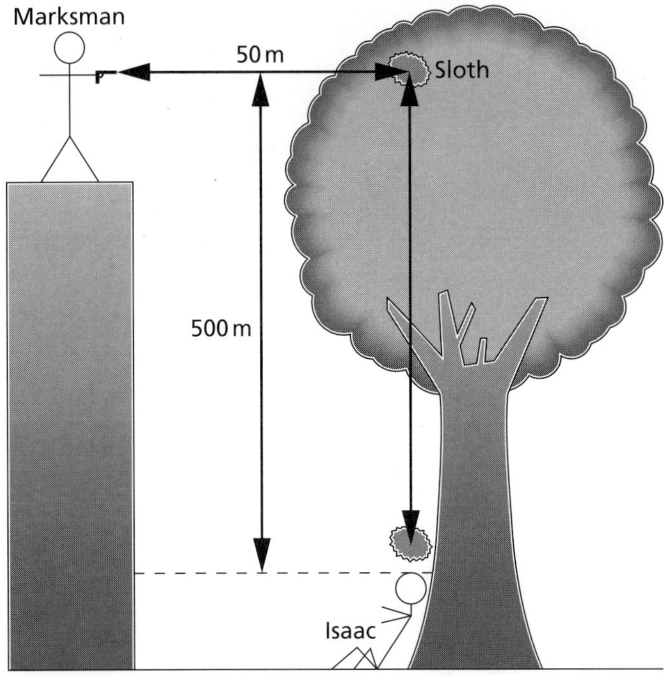

A lively young marksman is about to practise his aim on a sloth (minding its own business in a tree which is ridiculously tall, even if it is a Canadian redwood). Isaac, an enthusiastic young botanist is sitting directly beneath the sloth, studying the local flora and fauna.

The bullet from the marksman's gun travels at a constant speed of 20 m/s (as he is only an amateur marksman, so hasn't got a proper gun yet).

1. *Assuming that the speed of sound is 331 m/s, how long to the nearest hundredth of a second does it take for the sloth to hear the shot? (We are ignoring any air resistance.)* [2]

Using time = $\dfrac{\text{distance}}{\text{average speed}}$ *

$\dfrac{50}{331}$ = 0.15 s to 2 decimal places

It takes the sloth 0.15 seconds to hear the shot.*

Sadly, the noise frightens the sloth, and it loses its grip. Accelerating at 9.8 m/s^2 due to gravity, it rapidly approaches Isaac's head.

2. *How long does it take for the bullet to travel the 50 m horizontally, so that it is vertically above Isaac's head?* [2]

time = $\dfrac{\text{distance}}{\text{average speed}} = \dfrac{50}{20}$ = 2.5 s*

The bullet takes 2.5 seconds.*

3. *Allowing for the sloth's delayed fall, how far has the sloth fallen by this time?* [3]

Time the sloth falls for before the bullet travels 50 m
= 2.5 – 0.15 s
= 2.35 s *

Using $s = ut + \frac{1}{2}at^2$ *
$s = 0 + (\frac{1}{2} \times 9.8 \times 2.35^2)$ *
$s = 27.06$ m

The sloth has fallen 27.06 m after 2.35 s.*

4. *Does the bullet hit the sloth, and if not, how much does it miss by?* [3]

After 2.5 s, the bullet has fallen s metres:
$s = ut + \frac{1}{2}at^2$ *
$s = 0 + (\frac{1}{2} \times 9.8 \times 2.5^2)$ *
$s = 30.63$ m.

The bullet is therefore 30.63 m below the tree.*

The sloth has only fallen 27.06 m by this time, so the bullet misses the sloth by:
30.63 – 27.06 = 3.57 m*

5. *If the bullet had hit the sloth a mere 1 m above Isaac's head, which would have given him a fright, how far away from the tree would the marksman need to have been standing? Ignore the time taken for the sloth to hear the shot.* [7]

(This is probably a little too difficult for a GCSE paper, but if you can do it, any GCSE questions ought to be a doddle. Plus, we're just setting a good example to GCSE examiners.)

To find the time taken for the sloth to fall to 1 m above Isaac's head:

Distance the sloth falls = 500 – 1 = 499 m*
Acceleration (due to gravity) = 9.8 m/s^2 *

Using $s = ut + \frac{1}{2}at^2$ *
as $u = 0$, $ut = 0$
$\therefore s = \frac{1}{2}at^2$ *

$$t^2 = \frac{s}{\frac{1}{2}a}$$

$$\Rightarrow t = \sqrt{\frac{s}{\frac{1}{2}a}}$$

$$t = \sqrt{\frac{499}{0.5 \times 9.8}}$$

$t = 10.1$ s*

Thus the bullet would have travelled for 10.1 seconds.

Horizontal distance travelled by bullet:

$s = ut + \frac{1}{2}at^2$ *
$s = (20 \times 10.1) + 0$
$s = 202$ m.

Thus the marksman would have needed to be 202 m away from the tree to hit the sloth 1 m above Isaac's head.*

A trailer is hanging over the edge of a cliff. The trailer contains £70 million of gold bullion, and four people.
The centre of mass of the gold is 2 m beyond the edge of the cliff.
The trailer, weighing 1 tonne (excluding the gold and people), has a centre of gravity 25 cm horizontally to the left of the cliff edge.
The four people are 2.5 m from the cliff edge.
Assume that the gold is worth £140 per gram.
The trailer is completely stationary, i.e. it is in equilibrium.
Assume gravitational field strength to be 10 N/kg.

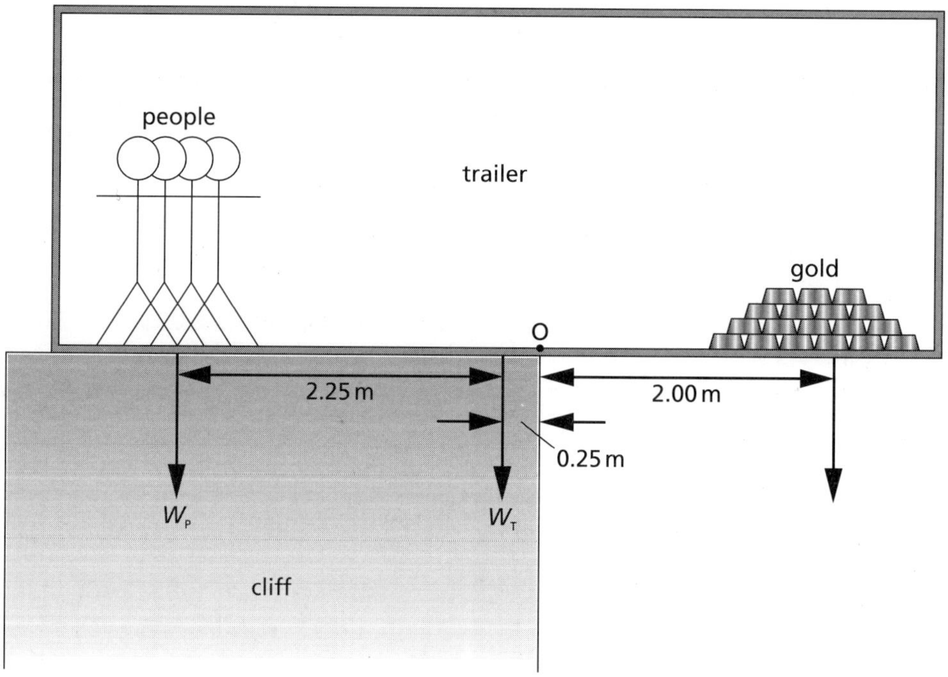

6. *Find the mass of the gold.* [1]

$$\text{Mass} = \frac{70\,000\,000}{140} = 500\,000 \text{ g} = 500 \text{ kg}$$

(The answer has been converted to SI units for convenience later.)

7. *Find the total weight of the four people.* [7]

As the trailer is in equilibrium:
Total clockwise moment about point O = total anticlockwise moment about point O*

$\therefore$ moment of gold about point O = moment of people about point O + moment of trailer about point O*

Using $W = mg$, the force exerted by gold due to its weight:
500×10
$= 5000$ N *

Moment = Fd, where F is force (weight) and d is the distance from the pivot (cliff edge)
So the moment of the gold is:
5000×2
$= 10\,000$ Nm *

Therefore:
$\text{Moment}_{\text{people}} + \text{Moment}_{\text{trailer}} = 10\,000$ N m

As the trailer has a mass of 1 tonne (1000 kilograms), if the weight of the people is W_p:
$(W_p \times 2.5) + (1000 \times 10 \times 0.25) = 10\,000$*
$2.5W_p = 10\,000 - 2500$
$= 7500$

Thus, weight of people $= \frac{7500}{2.5}$
$= 3000$ N*

(Note: not 300 kg! kgs are mass.)

8. *Find the mean mass of one person.* [2]

Total weight = 3000 N

Mean weight $= \frac{3000}{4}$ (since there are four people) = 750 N*

Therefore:

Mean mass $= \frac{750}{10} = 75$ kg*

($W = mg$, therefore $m = \frac{W}{g}$)

The asterisk (*) shows where individual marks are awarded in multiple mark questions. You can see it pays to write your working even if you can't reach a final answer. Naturally you won't get full marks without the final answer, but you might only lose one mark if the rest of your working can be seen.

topic two

waves

Describing and measuring waves

Waves move energy from one place to another. Particles forming the wave do not change their average position. Energy travels along the wave. You can see this on a Slinky spring. When you send a wave down it, the energy passes from each coil to the next, but each one maintains its average position.

There are two distinct types of wave:

Longitudinal the oscillation is in the same direction as the movement of energy, e.g. sound. The most dramatic examples of longitudinal waves are seismic **P waves** in earthquakes, and a good way to remember that the P waves are longitudinal is to think of the waves as being **P**ushed forwards and **P**ulled backwards

Transverse oscillation is perpendicular to the movement of energy, e.g. light waves. The most dramatic examples are **S waves**, again to do with seismology, and you can remember this by thinking of transverse waves as being **S**haken **S**ide to **S**ide

Both of these can be demonstrated using the Slinky spring:
A Slinky spring is laid out on the floor. If you shake it from side to side, then you get a transverse wave. If you push it, and then pull it, you get a longitudinal wave.

A diagram of a transverse wave (a graph of displacement against distance) is shown below. Each point on the wave is oscillating at 90° to the direction of the wave.

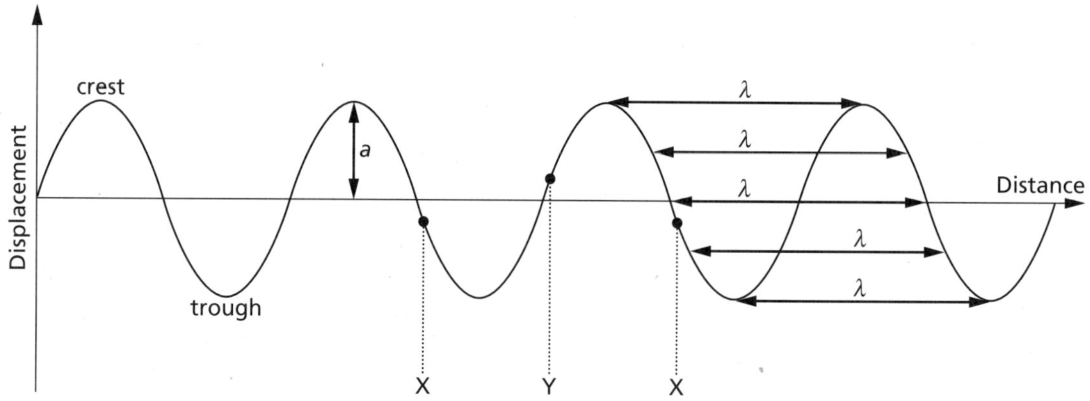

a is the **amplitude**, i.e. the maximum displacement of any point from the equilibrium position. The equilibrium is where displacement = 0, and so this is the average position of any point on the wave. λ ('lambda') is the **wavelength**, which is the distance from crest to crest, and trough to trough.

Two points that are in phase are one wavelength apart.
X and X are at the same point in their paths and are moving in the same direction; they are **in phase**. X and Y are exactly **out of phase**.

Time period this is the time for one point to go through one complete cycle of oscillation, and it is called T

Frequency the number of cycles of oscillation per second of a point

$$\text{Frequency} = \frac{1}{\text{time period}}$$

$$f = \frac{1}{T}$$

f frequency or cycles per second (hertz (Hz))
T time period (s)

In a sound wave, the **pitch** depends on frequency: the higher the frequency, the higher the pitch. **Loudness** depends on amplitude: the greater the amplitude, the louder the sound.

The wave equation

$$\text{Speed} = \text{frequency} \times \text{wavelength}$$

$$v = f\lambda$$

v speed of wave (m/s)
f frequency (Hz)
λ wavelength (m)

Ripple tank pictures: reflection and refraction

A ripple tank is a shallow glass tray with dippers to make waves, which can be straight ('plane') or circular. The tank is illuminated, so that you can see the waves projected onto a screen.

Reflection in a plane 'mirror'

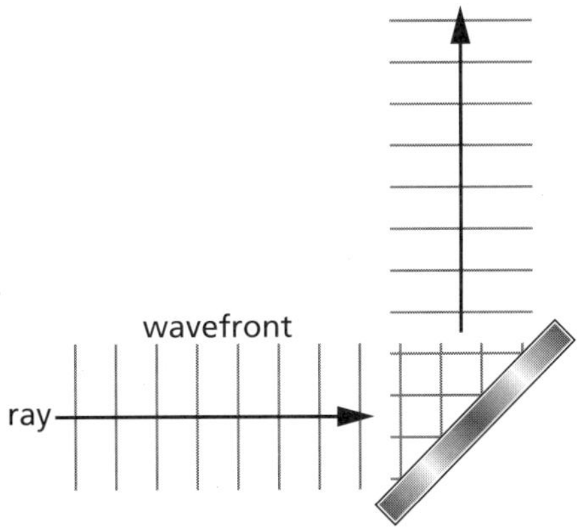

The diagram shows straight (plane) waves hitting a straight (plane) reflector.

The wavefronts are lines drawn to represent the crests of the waves. Each line is one wavelength from the next. Imagine ripples in water: these are the wavefronts. The 'ray' is the line through the wavefronts (the arrow) which represents the direction of movement of the wave.

Refraction

If you put a glass block in the ripple tank, just below the surface, the water becomes even shallower. In shallow water, the waves travel more slowly and the wavelength becomes smaller (since the frequency remains the same).

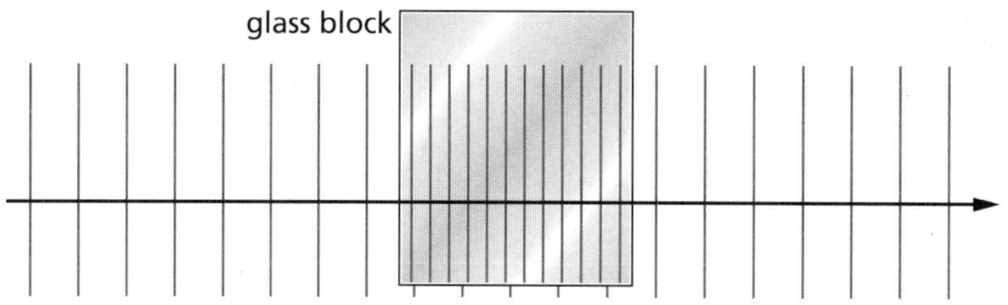

Normal a line drawn at 90° to a boundary

In the diagram below, the glass block has been turned so that the wavefronts are no longer parallel to the boundary between the deeper and shallower water. (The direction of the waves is not normal to the boundary.) As the waves slow down, they are refracted towards the normal. As the waves speed up, going from shallow water to deep water, they are refracted away from the normal.

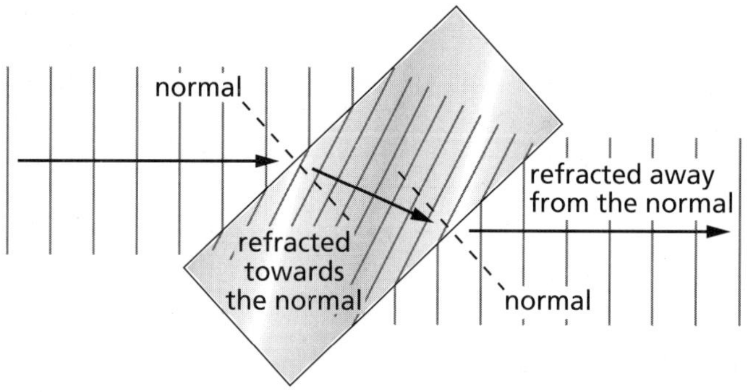

Note that if the sides of the block are parallel, the angle through which the waves bend towards the normal on entry is the same as the angle through which they bend away from the normal on exit. (See ray diagrams in topic three, optics.)

Special properties of waves: diffraction and interference

Diffraction spreading out of waves after passing through a narrow gap, or past a corner

Light diffracts, as it is a wave motion. (It is also a particle motion, but forget about quantum physics for now.) Diffraction is most obvious when the size of the gap is approximately equal to the wavelength of the wave. Note that the wave's wavelength does not change after it is diffracted

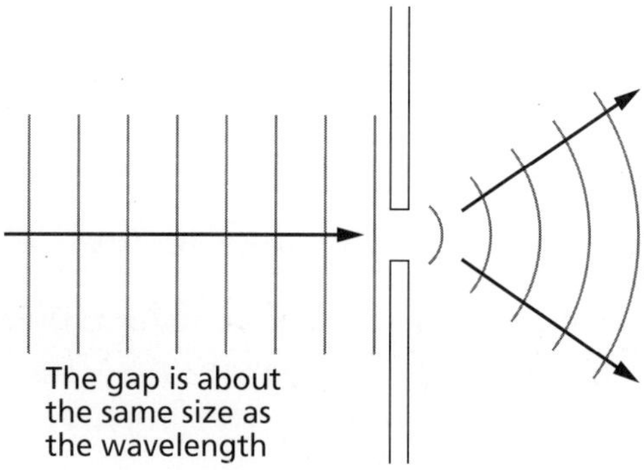

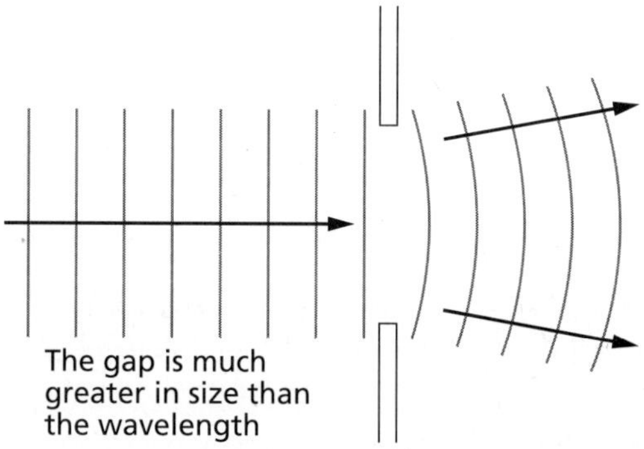

Interference the effect produced when similar waves reinforce or cancel each other out, either totally or partially

Constructive interference

Waves arrive in phase, and produce a wave with a larger amplitude, e.g. crest plus crest. If two identical waves arrive together exactly in phase, then the resulting wave has the same frequency, but twice the amplitude.

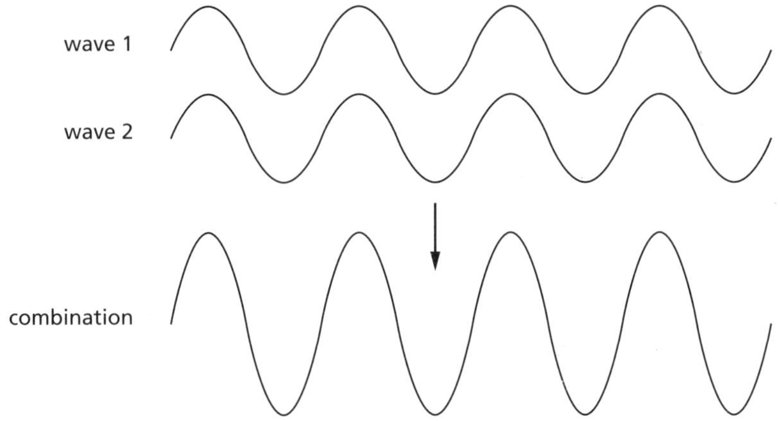

Destructive interference

Waves arrive out of phase, and cancel out, e.g. crest plus trough.

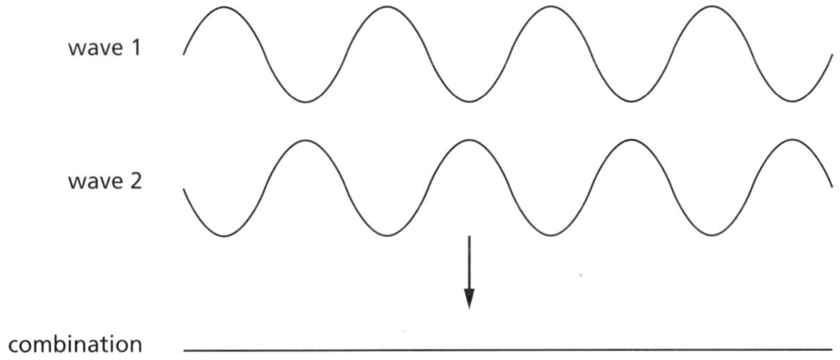

The electromagnetic spectrum

The electromagnetic spectrum includes radio waves, microwaves, infrared light, visible light, ultraviolet light, X-rays and gamma rays.

'Electromagnetic' means that the waves are oscillations in electric and magnetic fields. These fields are 'vibrating' at right angles to each other.

Properties of electromagnetic waves:

- They transfer energy.
- They are all transverse (unless you are doing degree level physics!).
- They can be reflected, refracted and diffracted.
- They can travel in a vacuum.
- They all travel in a vacuum at the same speed of 300 000 000 m/s (the speed of light).
- The higher the frequency (i.e. the shorter the wavelength), the greater the energy.
- The absorption of electromagnetic waves increases the temperature of the absorbing body and vibrates free charges at the frequency of the wave.

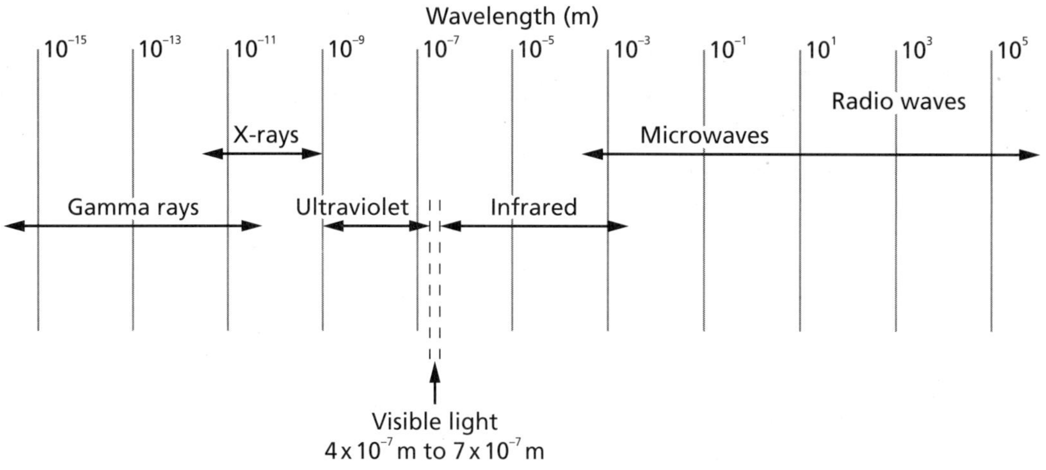

Visible light occupies only a very small fraction of the electromagnetic spectrum. Red has the longest wavelength of visible light, and blue has the shortest wavelength.

Polarisation

An electromagnetic wave has electric and magnetic fields vibrating at right angles to the direction of motion. However, this wave could be vertical, or horizontal, or any other angle, i.e. the wave is vibrating in many different planes.

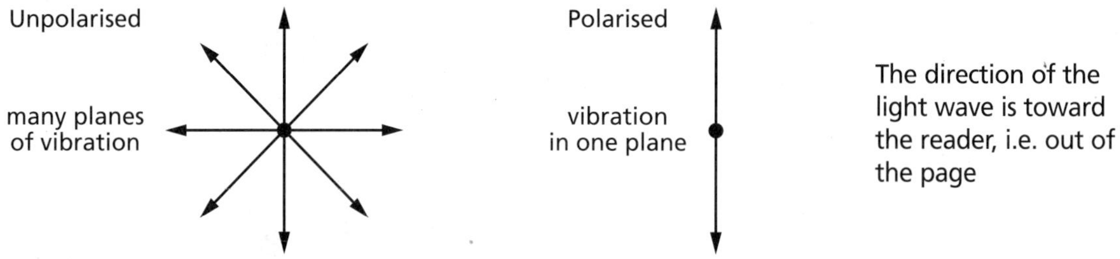

Certain materials have a special property; they are said to be able to polarise waves. A polarising material only lets light through that is vibrating in one particular plane. If you pass a light wave through such a substance, then it will absorb part of the light.

The polarisation plane depends on the electric field.

When light is reflected, it is partly polarised. Say it is reflected off snow. Much of the light is vibrating in the same plane. A pair of Polaroid® sunglasses is intended to cut out light that is vibrating in that particular plane, and so reduce the glare from the reflection.

You cannot polarise longitudinal waves.

Sound

Sound is caused by vibrations, which alternately compress, then decompress the particles in the medium (e.g. air, water) which carries the wave. A longitudinal wave is produced, and the vibrating particles transfer energy.

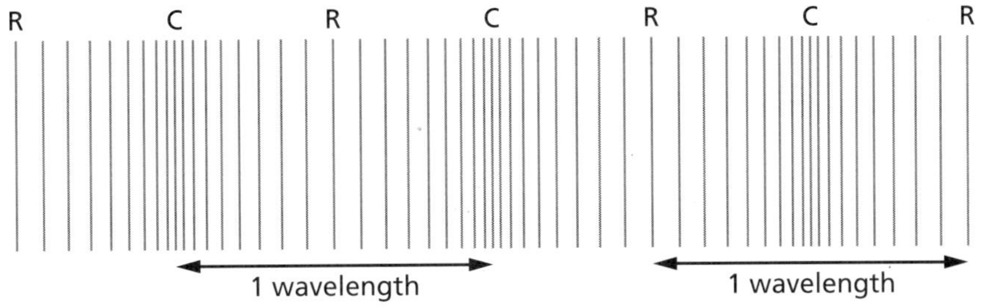

C, compressions
R, rarefactions (areas of decompression)

Going back to the Slinky spring model, the areas where the rings of the spring are close together are the compressed areas, the areas where the rings are further apart are the rarefactions.

The wavelength is the distance between a pair of compressions or rarefactions.

The wave equation, $v = f\lambda$, applies to sound waves.

Sound requires a medium, a substance whose particles vibrate, and carry the wave. So sound cannot travel in a vacuum.

The speed of sound in air is less than the speed of sound in a liquid, which is less than the speed of sound in a solid. This is because sound travels faster through a medium whose particles are more closely bound together.

(Speed of sound in air at 0°C ~331 m/s; speed of sound in air at room temp. ~340 m/s.)

The speed of sound is much lower than the speed of light, and so in a thunderstorm you see the lightning before you hear the thunder.

Echoes these are reflected sound waves

Ultrasound sound of a frequency which is too high for humans to hear, i.e. above 20 kHz

In sonar depth-finding an ultrasonic pulse is transmitted to the seabed and is reflected back. Because we know the speed of sound in water, we can work out the distance to the seabed, and figure out its shape. Ultrasound is also used in prenatal scanning, and to clean delicate mechanisms without taking them apart.

The ear

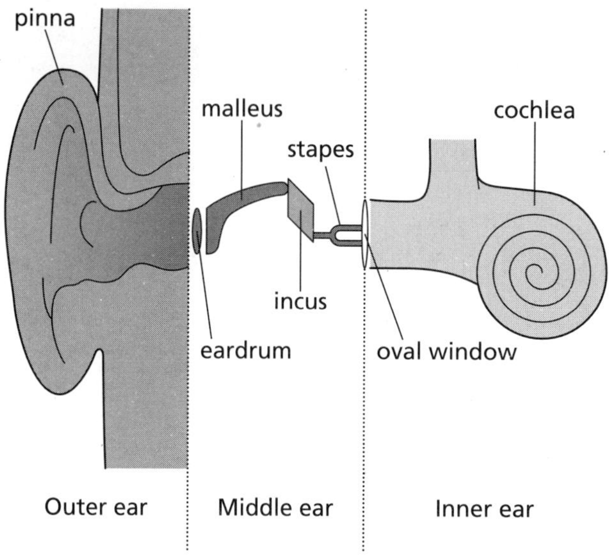

Sound waves are collected by the **pinna** (the bit some people can wiggle). They travel along to the eardrum, which vibrates. Vibrations carry on to the three bones, the **malleus** (hammer), then the **incus** (anvil), then the **stapes** (stirrup). The bones are arranged so that they form a lever to magnify the force. The stapes vibrates, and pushes on the oval window. The **cochlea** (a spirally snail-like bit, that contains fluid) receives the vibrations. Vibrations are converted to nervous impulses that travel along a nerve to the brain, which interprets them.

Hearing range of a young child: 20 Hz – 20 000 Hz
As you get older, the upper limit of your hearing range decreases.

Resonance

The **natural frequency** of an object is the frequency at which it vibrates when you tap it. If you apply a forced frequency to an object, which just so happens to be that natural frequency, the object starts to vibrate at that frequency, but with a much larger amplitude. This phenomenon is called **resonance**.

For example, a singer can smash a wine glass if she sings at the right pitch. On a windy day in 1940, in the USA, the Tacoma Narrows bridge began to sway violently because its natural frequency was the same as the frequency at which the wind caused it to vibrate. Eventually the amplitude of the sway was so big that the bridge collapsed.

Pitch, timbre and loudness

Pitch depends on frequency.
Loudness depends on amplitude.
The timbre, or quality of sound, of a musical instrument depends on the waveform.

Basically, if the waveform is smooth, it sounds like a tuning fork, but if it is jagged, it sounds like *Smells Like Teen Spirit* by Nirvana on a bad day. The waveform from a tuning fork is much smoother than the waveform from a violin, which has a more complicated combination of frequencies.

Worked Questions

A sound wave, of wavelength 129 cm is travelling in air. Assume the speed of sound is 330 m/s.

1. *What is the frequency of the wave? (Give your answer to three significant figures)* [2]

   Answer:
   Using $v = f\lambda$ where v = velocity (m/s)
   f = frequency (Hz)
   λ = wavelength (m);

   Note the unit conversion here
   ↓
   129 cm = 1.29 m

   thus $f = v/\lambda$

   $f = 330/1.29 = 256$ Hz

   Bonus: This is the frequency of which musical note?
   Answer: 'middle C'

A glass is known to have a natural frequency of 2500 Hz. A singer nearby coincidentally begins to sing at 2.5 kHz.

2. *Describe what happens to the glass when she sings.* [2]

   Answer:
   The glass will begin to resonate. It vibrates, with an extremely large amplitude, and may even shatter. (Notice how we're using key words? The examiners are looking for the word *resonates*, or *resonance*, and something about a large *amplitude*. The fact that the glass may shatter is only a minor point.)

The diagram below shows waves approaching a glass block in a ripple tank.

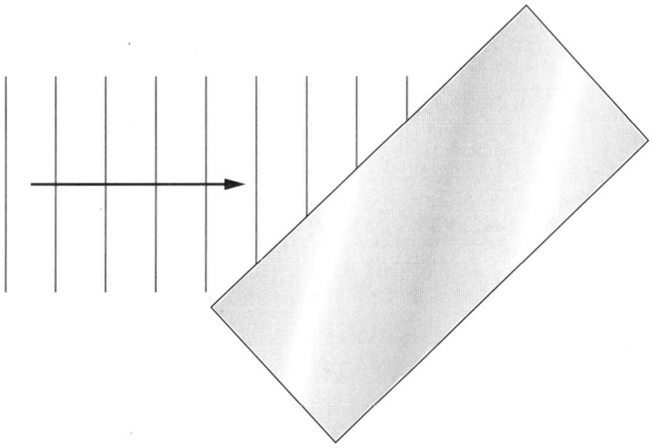

3. *Sketch the path of the waves on the diagram, when the glass block is placed at an angle (as shown) to the waves.* [4]

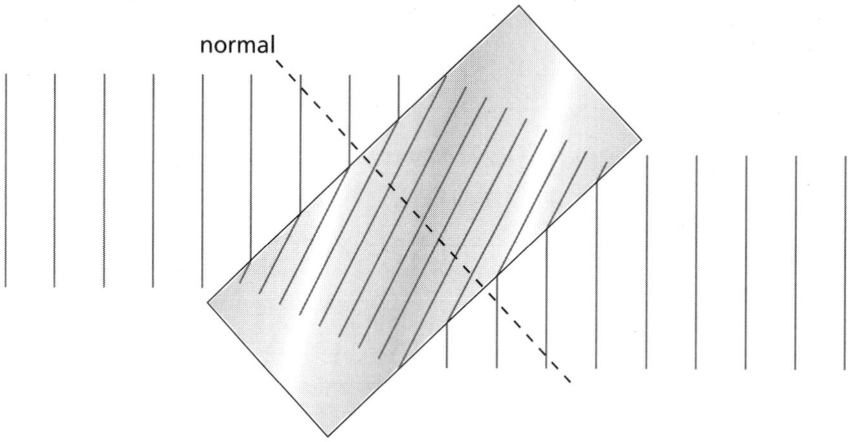

There are 3 marks for showing the waves changing their direction (correctly, towards the normal going into the shallower water above the glass block, away from the normal when leaving the shallower water over the block), 1 mark for showing that the wavefronts are closer together inside the glass block. (i.e. the wavelength is smaller).

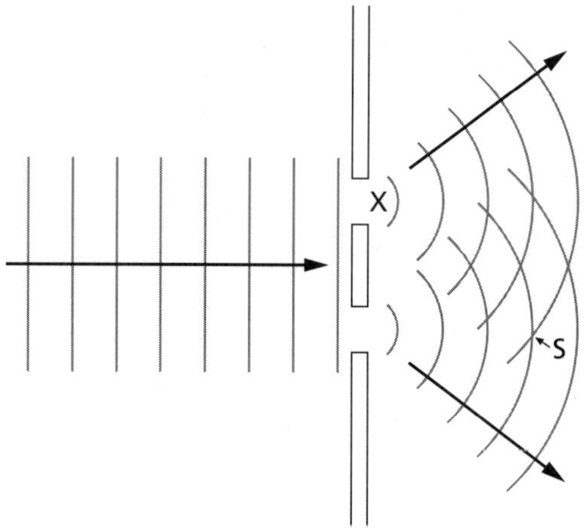

1. *Name the effect occurring at X.* [1]

   Answer:
   Diffraction.

2. *What effect is occurring at point S ?* [1]

   Answer:
   Constructive interference. S is a point where two crests meet and accentuate each other.
   (Far too easy, but our imagination was running out.)

optics

Light is an electromagnetic wave and travels at 3×10^8 m/s (300 000 000 m/s) in a vacuum. Visible light has wavelengths in the range 4×10^{-7} m to 7×10^{-7} m.

1 light year is the distance light travels in a year.

*Light travels in straight lines. This is called **rectilinear propagation**.*

Shadows

Shadows are dark areas cast when light is shone at an object. Some of the light continues to travel past it, but some is blocked by the object, so you get a dark area where no light enters.

Umbra the completely dark area where no light reaches

Penumbra the fuzzy shadow where some of the light falls

Umbra shadows are usually formed when the light source is small compared with the object. For instance, in the diagrams below, a 'point' light source such as a small light bulb, gives only an umbra.

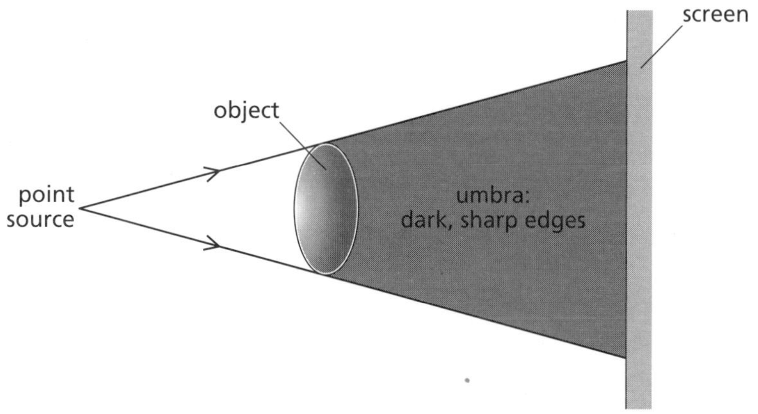

A large light source, such as a normal bulb, gives an umbra and a penumbra

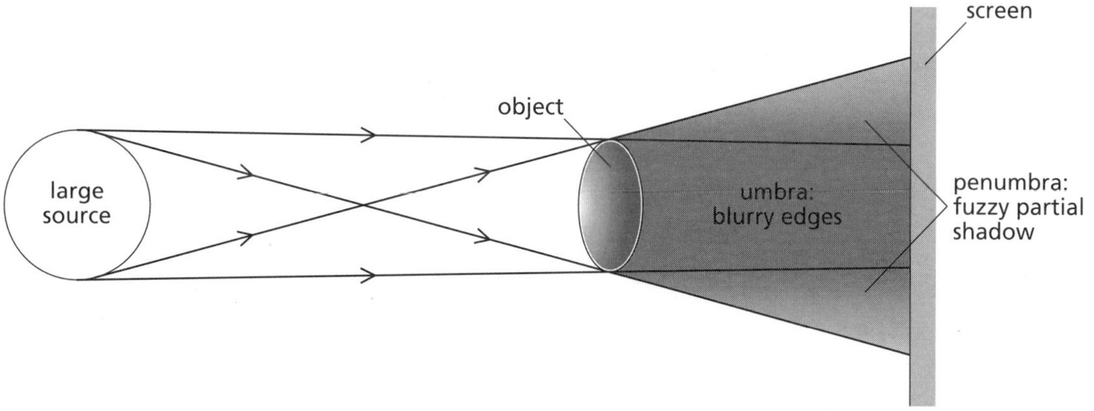

Reflection

Angle of incidence = angle of reflection
In symbols, the equation reads:

$\angle i = \angle r$

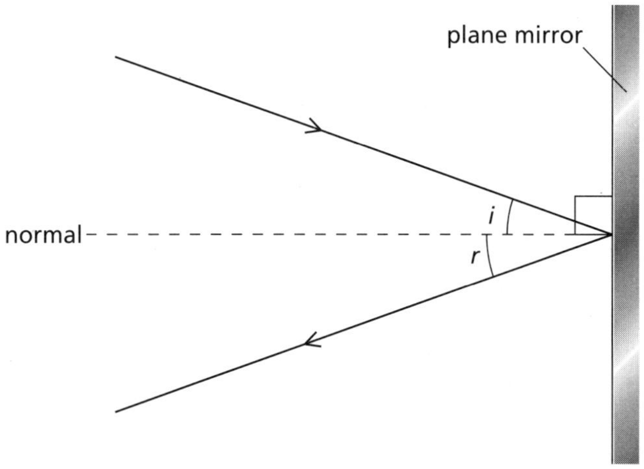

Image in a plane mirror

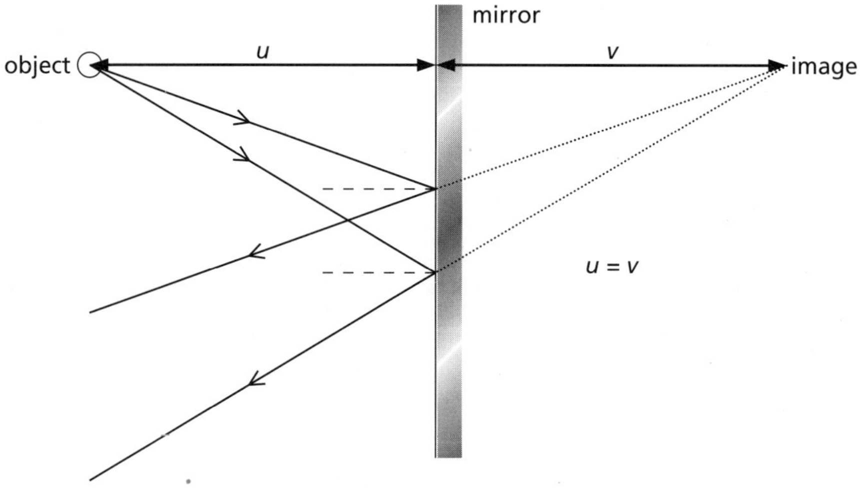

- The image is **virtual**: it is formed at a point which rays do not pass, but where the reflected rays appear to come from. The dotted lines show where the rays appear to come from, traced back to the image. A virtual image cannot be formed on a screen, unlike a real image.
- The image is **upright** but **laterally inverted**. In other words, the image is flipped back to front.
- It is the **same size as the object**.
- It is **the same distance behind the mirror as the object is in front**, or as shown in the diagram, $v = u$.

(You can make a ***real*** *image on a screen in a pinhole camera. The rays pass through a small hole, and the image is inverted left to right and upside-down. If the pinhole is made larger, the image is brighter, but becomes blurred.)*

Diffuse reflection

Reflection always occurs; that's how you can see things. Light reflects off objects and into your eye. Not all objects are shiny like a mirror because they aren't all smooth. Under a microscope you can see that most things are very rough, so you wouldn't expect them to reflect light like a mirror. Each different bit of surface is at a different angle, so light is reflected off at different angles.

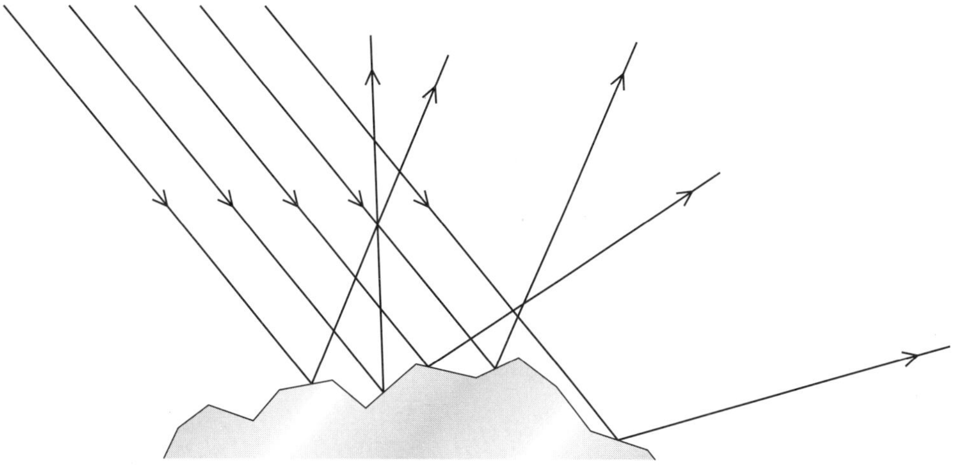

Refraction

When light enters an optically more dense medium, it slows down. When light enters a less optically dense medium, it speeds up.

If the light enters at an angle, the change in speed makes it change direction.

Say you happen to be driving a double-decker bus in the Sahara, and one wheel happens to get stuck in quicksand. That side slows down, so the bus turns, and is refracted towards the quicksand. (Thank goodness for Physics, at least we'll know why there's a problem in that situation.)

When light enters an optically more dense medium it is refracted towards the normal. When light enters an optically less dense medium it is refracted away from the normal.

(Some of the light, when meeting glass, water, or anything else transparent, will be reflected.)

Refractive index a measure of how much a substance causes light to bend

The refractive index is a ratio of the two speeds of light. It has no units.

$$\text{Refractive index of substance} = \frac{\text{speed of light in vacuum}}{\text{speed of light in substance}}$$

In the following diagram a ray is entering a more dense medium, for example going from air into a glass block.
The ray is refracted towards the normal.

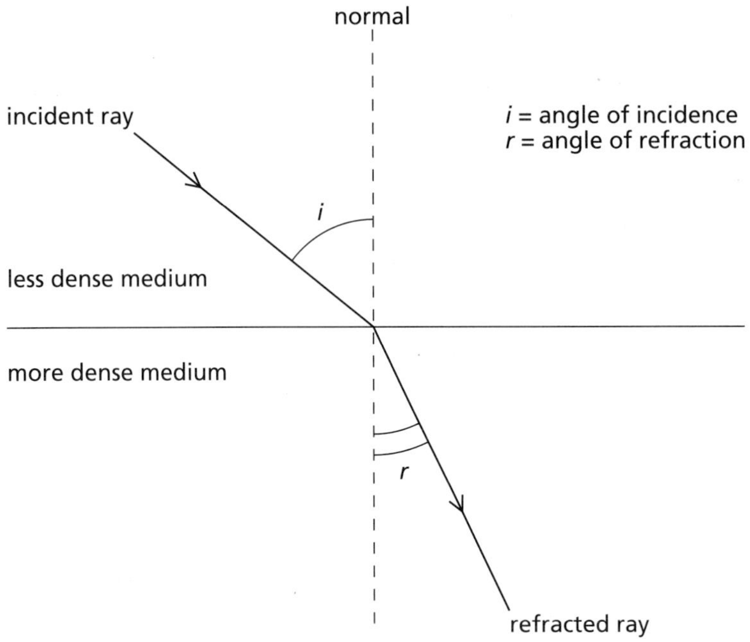

The angle of incidence is *i*, and the angle of refraction is *r*.

Real and apparent depth

$$\text{Refractive index} = \frac{\text{real depth}}{\text{apparent depth}}$$

Rays from underwater are refracted away from the normal (entering a less dense medium). They end up so that they appear to be coming from a point that is not as deep as their actual source.

Real depth > apparent depth.

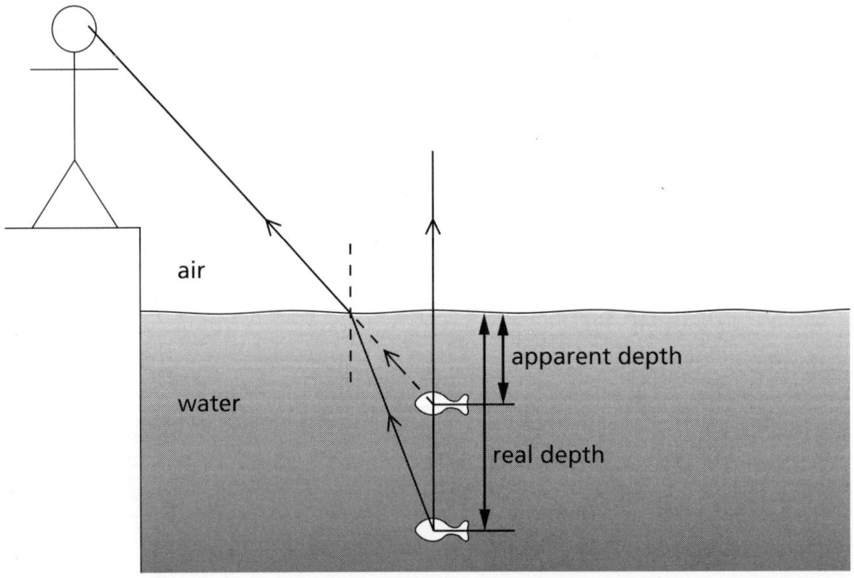

Total internal reflection

Refraction in a semicircular glass block

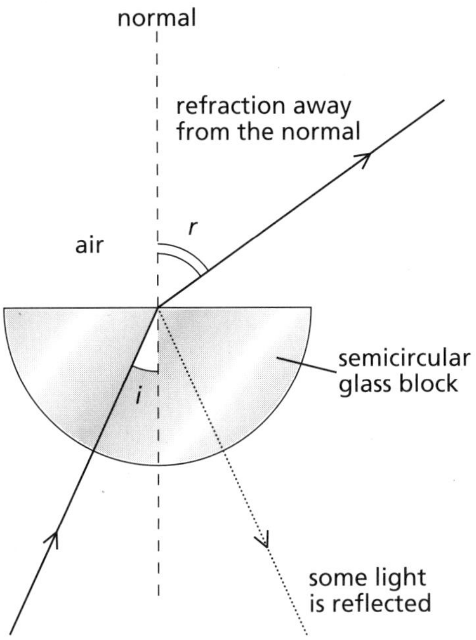

The ray enters the glass block at 90° to the surface, i.e. normally, so it isn't refracted at that point. When the ray leaves the glass block, it is entering a less dense medium, i.e. air. The ray is therefore refracted away from the normal. There is partial internal reflection, as some of the light is reflected by the glass.

The critical case

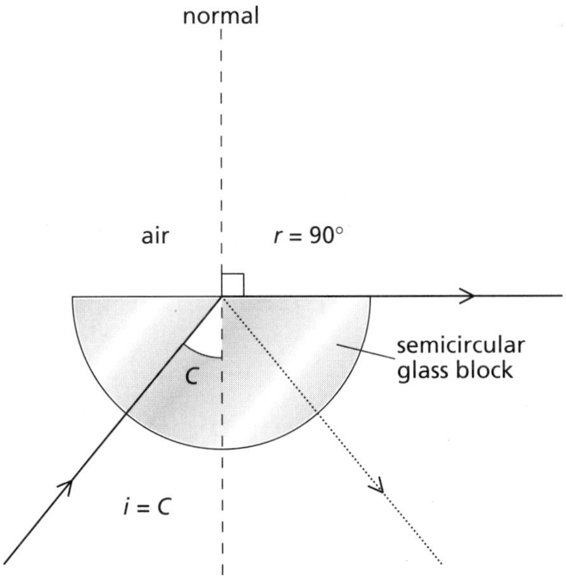

The critical angle *C* is the angle of incidence where the angle of refraction is at 90° to the normal. *C* for glass is approximately 42°.

When *i* is greater than the critical angle

If light from the more dense medium tries to enter the less dense medium in a situation where *i* is greater than the critical angle, then **total internal reflection occurs**. The light hits the boundary of the glass and air but it is all reflected back into the glass. The boundary acts like a mirror.

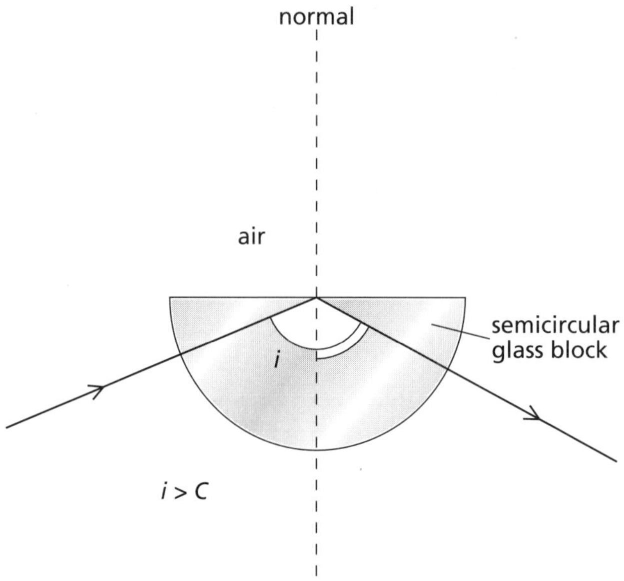

Uses of total internal reflection
Prisms as used in single-lens reflex cameras, and the optic fibres used in endoscopy and communications depend on total internal reflection.

Mirages
Mirages are caused by total internal reflection. When the air closer to the ground is hotter than the air above, the hot air is the less dense medium. Light entering it at an angle greater than the critical is reflected and the image of the sky looks like a pool of water.

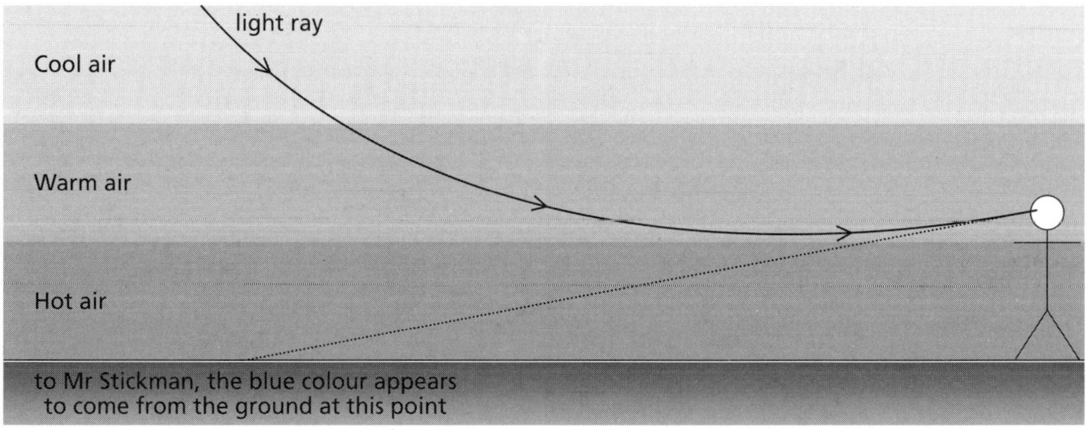

Lenses

There are two types of lens: **convex** and **concave**.

Convex lenses converge rays of light that are parallel to the principal axis to the principal focus PF. The image can be either magnified, diminished or the same size as the object.

Concave lenses diverge rays that are parallel to the principal axis so that they appear to come from the principal focus. The image is always diminished.

Focal length the distance from the principal focus to the optical centre of the lens

A thicker lens will have a shorter focal length than a thinner lens of the same glass type and equal diameter.

In the following diagrams, PF is the principal focus; 2PF is a point that is at twice the focal length.

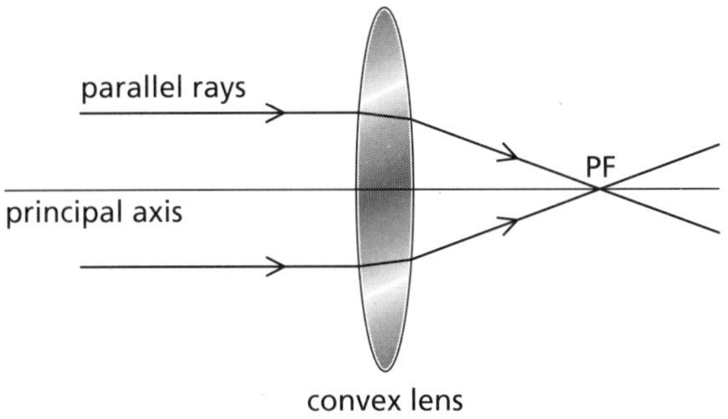

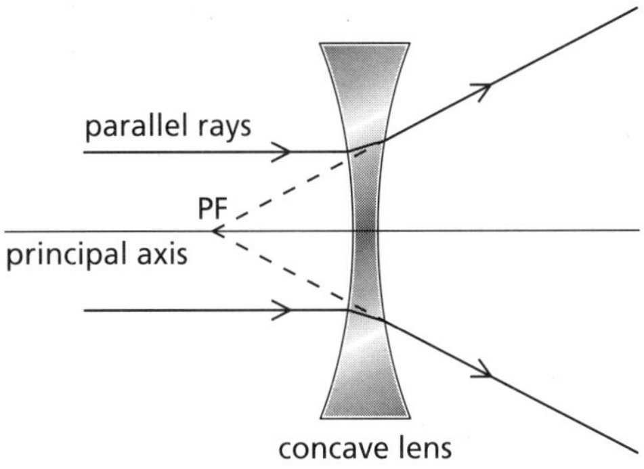

Drawing ray diagrams

If you need to draw a ray diagram for a convex lens, then you use the following three constructions:

1. Rays that are parallel to the **principal axis** are refracted through the **principal focus, PF**.

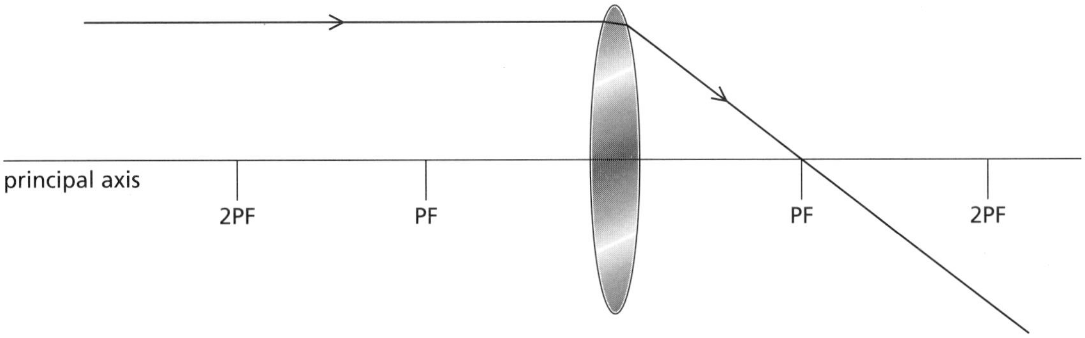

2. Rays of light passing through the **optical centre** of the lens travel straight on.

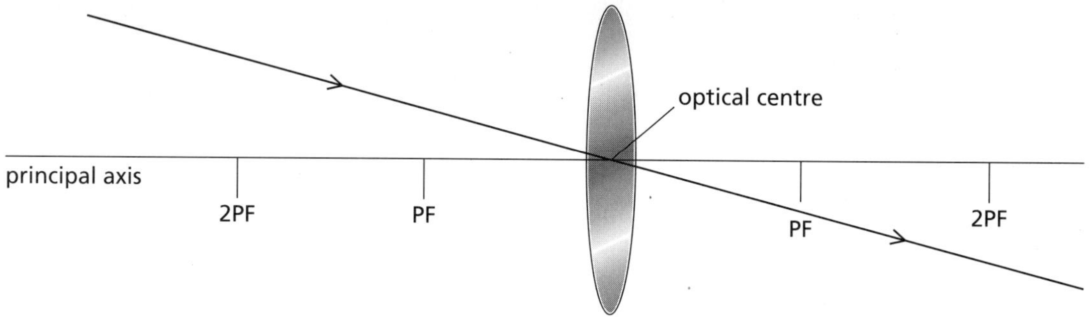

3. Rays of light passing through the principal focus of the lens are refracted parallel to the principal axis.

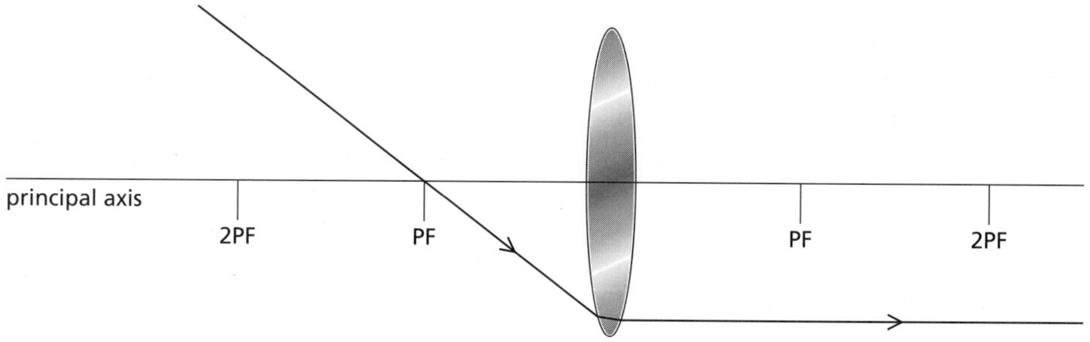

Images formed by a convex lens

The type of image depends on the position of the object. O is the object, I is its image.

1. Object beyond 2PF

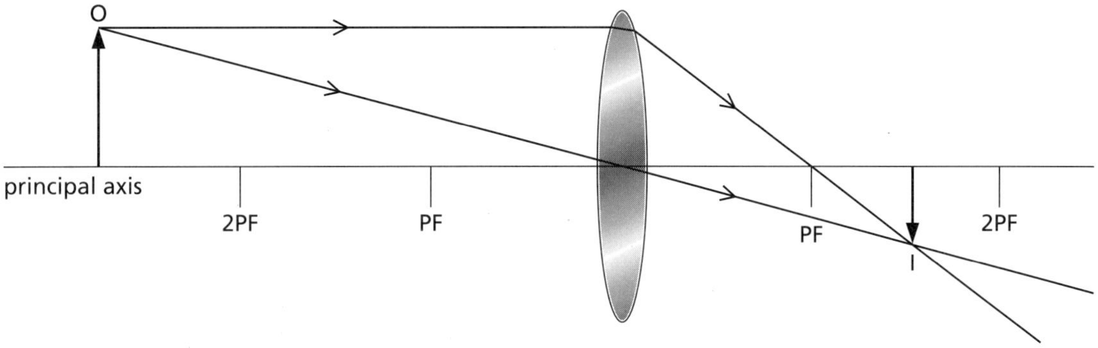

The image is between PF and 2PF, inverted, diminished and real. Cameras and eyes form this type of image.

A real image is one that can be formed on a screen.

2. Object between PF and 2PF

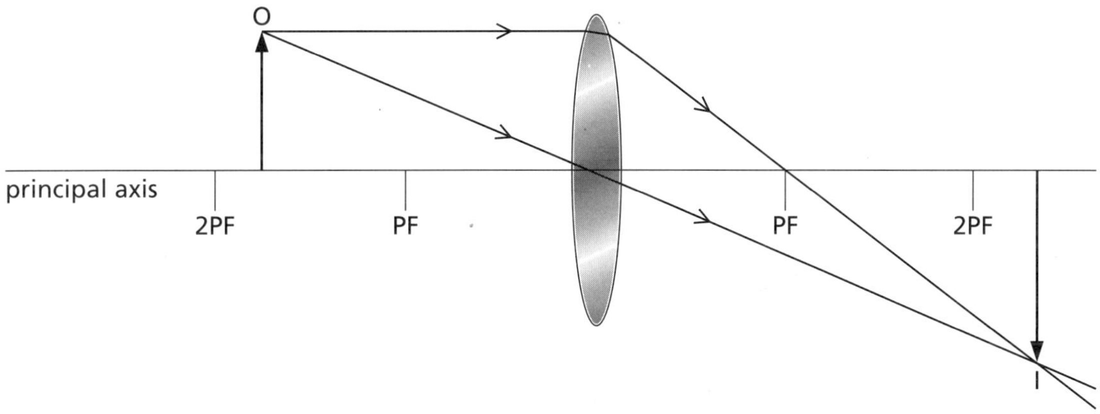

The image is beyond 2PF, inverted, real and magnified.
Slide and film projectors produce this type of image.

3. Between PF and lens

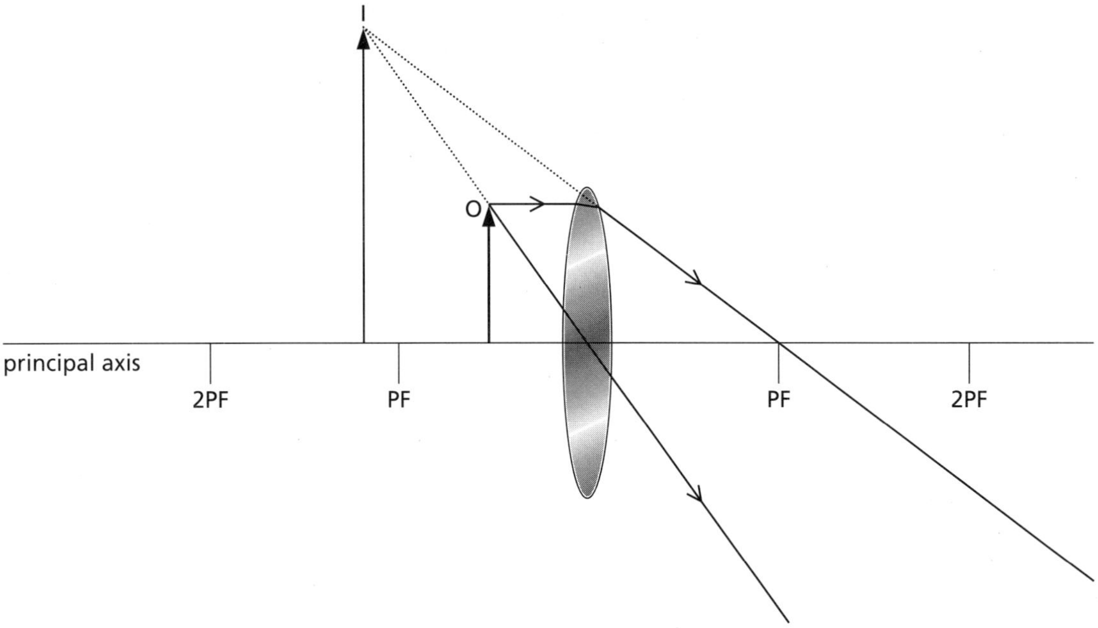

The image appears to be on the same side of the lens as the object, upright, virtual and magnified. These types of images are formed by magnifying glasses, the eye lenses in telescopes, and in spectacles prescribed for long sight.

A virtual image is one where the rays do not actually originate from where they appear to, and the image cannot be formed on a screen.

Magnification

$$\text{Linear magnification} = \frac{\text{height of image}}{\text{height of object}} = \frac{\text{image distance}}{\text{object distance}}$$

Image distance distance between image and lens (m), usually given the symbol v

Object distance distance between object and lens (m), usually given the symbol u

Note that for virtual images, v *is negative.*

Calculating focal length

The focal length is f, in metres.

$$\frac{1}{f} = \frac{1}{v} + \frac{1}{u}$$

f focal length (m)
v image distance (m)
u object distance (m)

$$\text{Power of a lens} = \frac{1}{f}$$

units are dioptres when f is in metres

The formulae above may not be in your particular syllabus; check with your teacher.

The eye

Unlike a camera lens the position of the lens in the eye stays constant. The **cornea** mainly does the focussing. The **lens** does the **accommodation** (fine-tuning).

The **ciliary muscles** vary the thickness of the lens, and therefore its focal length. When the ciliary muscles contract, the lens becomes more rounded (thicker). When they relax, they make it thinner. The **iris** is like the aperture of a camera: it varies the amount of light entering through the **pupil**.

Long-sightedness

Long-sightedness happens because the light rays do not converge enough to form an image on the retina. The reasons for this may be:

- the eyeball is too short
- the cornea and lens do not converge the light rays enough
- the ciliary muscles do not contract enough, making the lens too thin.

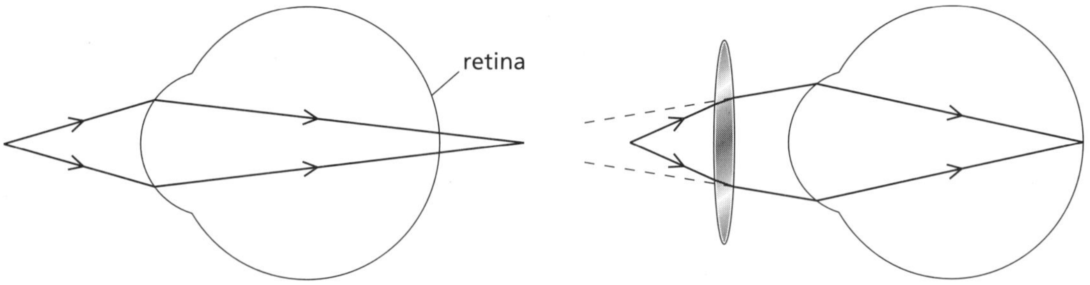

The correction is a convex lens, which helps the lens and the cornea converge the light rays, so that the image is focussed onto the retina.

Short-sightedness

Short-sightedness is caused by the image being formed in front of the retina. The reasons for this may be:

- the eyeball is too long
- the cornea and lens converge the light rays too much
- the ciliary muscles do not relax enough so the lens is too thick.

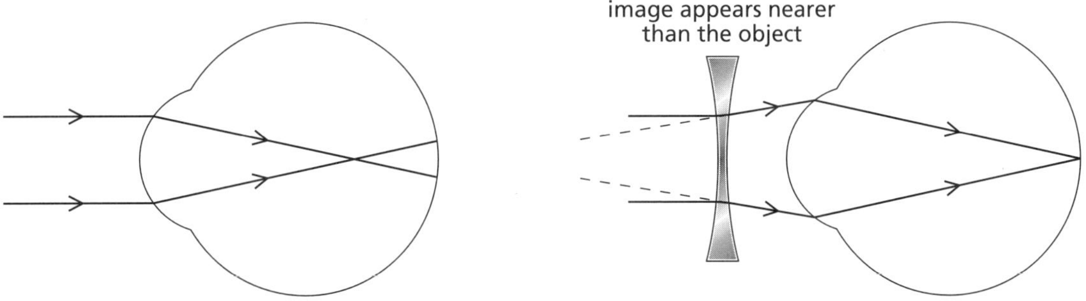

The correction is a concave lens. The image is being formed in front of the retina, so a concave lens diverges rays so that they can be converged again correctly by the eye lens and cornea onto the retina. You may have noticed that spectacle lenses do not curve inwards as in the diagram. They are, however, thick at the edges and thin in the centre.

Worked Questions

O is a beetle standing rigidly still whilst curiously staring at a convex lens.

1. *Draw in the appropriate rays to show where the image (which you will label I) of the beetle is formed.* [2]

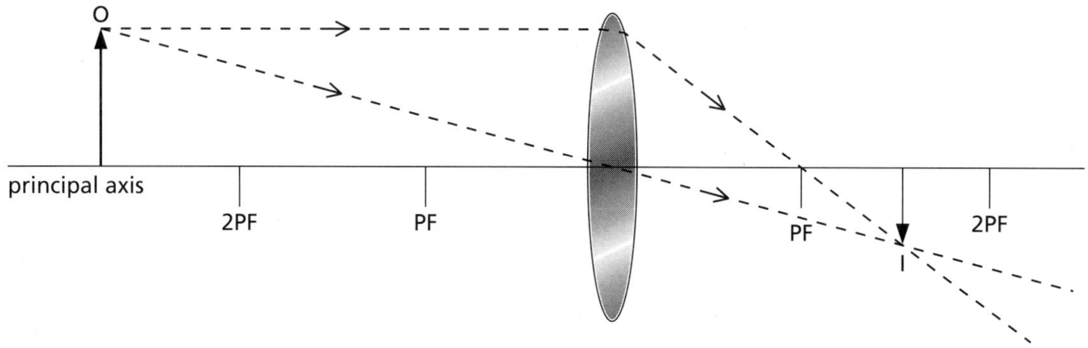

You get 1 mark for two of the three possible correct constructions to find the position of the image, and another for making sure that the image is diminished. You will be given most of what is shown in the diagram, i.e. you will only have to draw in the rays (shown here as dotted lines) and the letter I.

2. *Show, using a diagram, why objects placed within less than a focal length's distance from the convex lens produce a virtual image* [4]

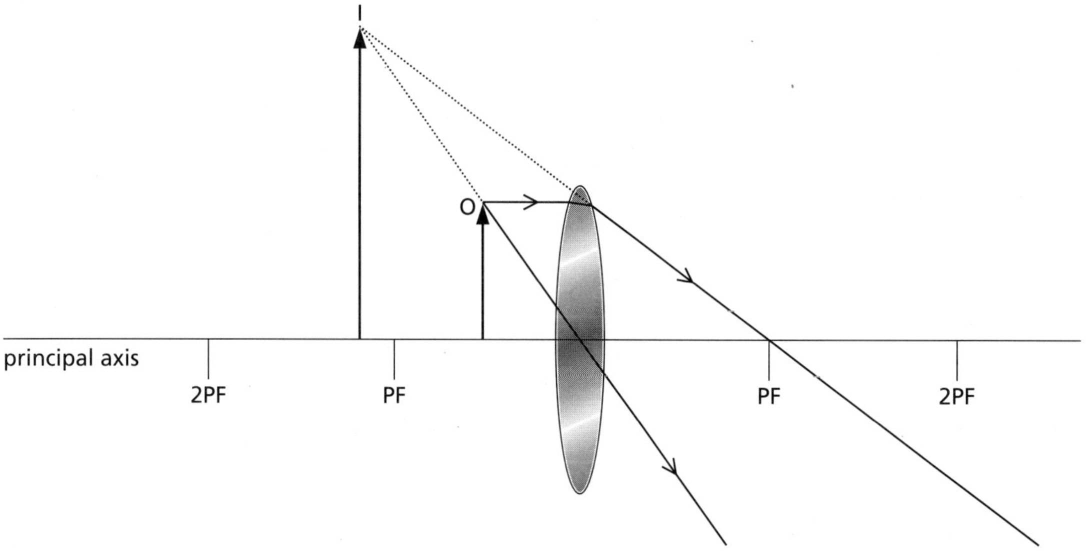

The diagram clearly shows that the position of the image is on the same side as the object, and dotted lines are used to represent the rays traced back to find the image.

3. Show, using diagrams, how glasses correct long- and short-sightedness. [8]

You get 2 marks per diagram, 1 each for the correct lens for the correct defect, and 2 for the accompanying waffle.

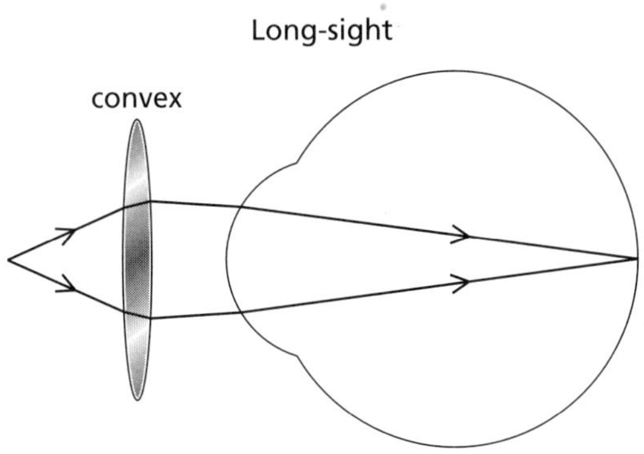

With long-sight, the light rays *do not converge enough* to form an *image on the retina*. Therefore, a *convex lens* is needed to help the *cornea and lens* to converge the rays.

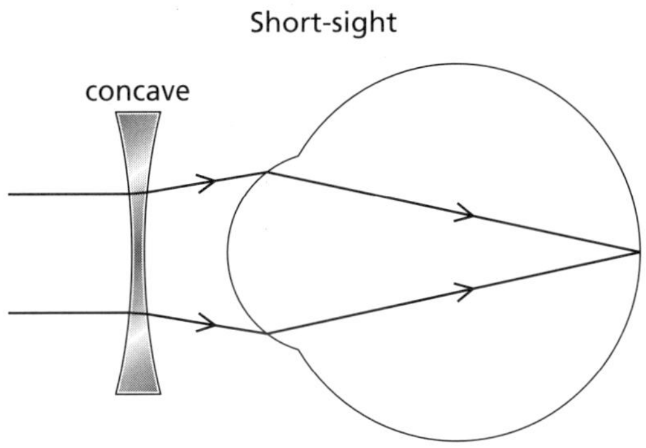

With short-sight, the *light rays converge too much* and form the *image before the retina*. Therefore, a *diverging concave* lens is needed to correct the problem.

The words in italic show points for which you automatically gain marks for if you write them down. As you can see with only two marks available for the written part, you could avoid fully answering the question but still receive most of the marks. If you have forgotten the exact answer, it pays just to spill whatever you know onto the page. Take note, this does not apply to all questions and this method should only be used in emergencies. It can backfire!

topic four
electricity

Static electricity

Static electricity is composed of **positive** and **negative charges**. In everyday circumstances, only the negative ones actually move around. The negative charge is carried by subatomic particles called **electrons**. (See topic eight, atomic structure, for more details.)

Like charges repel, opposite charges attract.

You can charge wool by rubbing it on polythene. Electrons are transferred off the wool to the polythene, so the polythene has extra electrons. This gives it a negative charge. The wool now has fewer electrons, and therefore a positive charge.

Electric circuits

In a **conductor** (any metal, or graphite) there are electrons that are free to move. These moving electrons form a **current**. Imagine that the conductor is a road, electrons are cars. **Insulators** have no free electrons to carry current. (Like trying to drive a wheel-clamped car.)

Current

Electricity travels by the easiest path, which is the one with least resistance.

Each electron has a negative charge.

Current a measure of how much charge passes a particular point every second, i.e. the **rate of flow of charge**

Current is measured in amperes (A), and is given the symbol I.

(Although electrons go from negative to positive, physicists (or were they chemists?) did not realise this at first, labelling diagrams with current going from positive to negative. However, nowadays this convention is still used, and in the case of certain semiconductors it can seem more appropriate. Don't worry about the direction of the electrons in exam questions unless you are asked specifically about it. Electrons go from negative to positive, but current (conventional current) goes from positive to negative. Always label your diagrams with conventional current direction.)

Charge

Charge is measured in coulombs (symbol Q).

1 coulomb the charge that flows when 1 ampere of current flows for 1 second of time

Charge = current × time

$Q = It$

Q coulombs (C)
I current (A)
t time (s)

Potential difference

The potential difference (p.d.) across a component in the circuit, is the amount of energy that the component converts from electrical to other forms, for every unit of charge that passes through it. For example, the p.d. across a bulb is the amount of electrical energy it converts to light and heat energy for every unit of charge that passes through its filament. The p.d. is measured in joules per coulomb, or volts. P.d. is sometimes referred to as **voltage**, although potential difference is technically better. As its name implies, it is the difference in potential between each end of a component.

Potential difference the energy converted from electrical energy, to other forms, per unit charge, by a component

$$\text{Potential difference} = \frac{\text{energy converted}}{\text{charge}}$$

$$p.d. = \frac{W}{Q}$$

p.d. volts (V)
W energy (J)
Q charge in coulombs (C)

1 joule per coulomb = 1 volt (1 V)

Series and parallel circuits

A series circuit is a circuit where there is one 'loop'.
A parallel circuit has more than one loop. Components are connected across each other (i.e. in parallel).
These two lamps are in series:

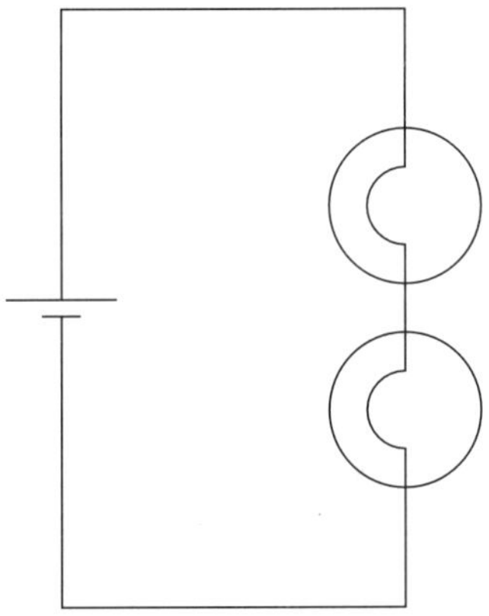

The total charge in a circuit will always stay constant, as electrons do not get lost. In a series circuit, all the electrons are in the same loop, so the current in a series circuit is the same all the way through.

In a series circuit, the current is the same throughout the circuit.

If the two lamps in the above series circuit were identical and they were connected to a 6 V supply, each lamp would have the same voltage of about 3 V across it.

These two lamps are in parallel:

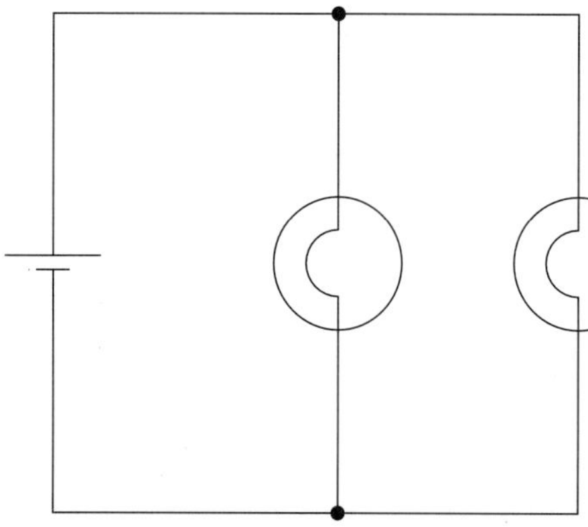

In parallel circuits, there is more than one loop. Electrons can effectively 'turn' in different directions at the junctions. So the current in one loop may be different from the current in another. But, again, no electrons are lost, so the total current in the circuit must be the sum of the currents in each loop.

Kirchhoff's First Law: *The total current flowing into a junction is the same as the sum of the currents flowing out of it.*

In a parallel circuit, each 'loop' is counted as a separate circuit. The two lamps above are in parallel. If they were both connected to a 6 V power supply, then each lamp would have a 6 V potential difference across it.

Resistance

All components in a circuit oppose the flow of current (including the wires, but this is taken to be negligible). Considering a metal: it is a structure of ions, held together by a 'sea' of electrons. The electrons, when carrying current, can bump into these ions. This opposes the flow of current. This opposition to current is called resistance. It is given the symbol R, and is measured in ohms (Ω).

Resistance is defined by the equation:

$$\text{Resistance} = \frac{\text{potential difference}}{\text{current}}$$

$$R = \frac{V}{I}$$

$$V = IR$$

R	resistance of component	ohms (Ω)
V	p.d. across component	volts (V)
I	current through component	amperes (A)

Graphs of potential difference, or voltage, against current

A graph of p.d. against current for a metal resistor would be a straight line through the origin. Its resistance stays constant. However, the same graph for a lamp filament is curved, as the increase in temperature also brings about an increase in resistance. Components whose resistance stays constant, so that the graph of p.d. against current is a straight line through the origin, are called **ohmic resistors**.

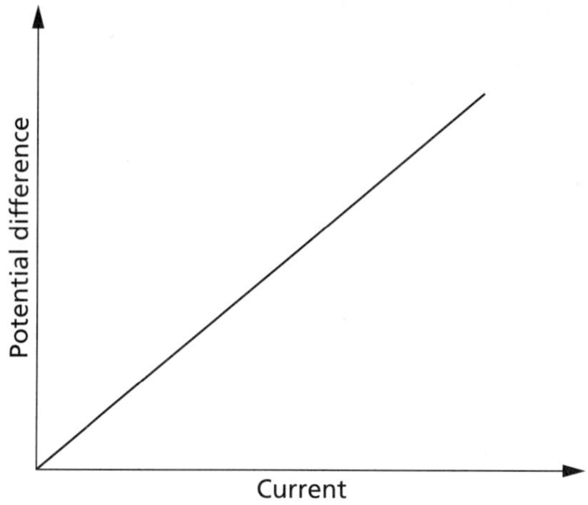

p.d. against current for an ohmic metal resistor at constant temperature

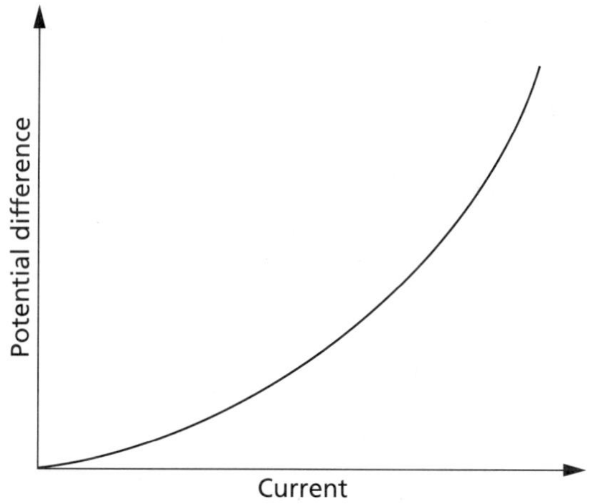

p.d. against current for a lamp filament

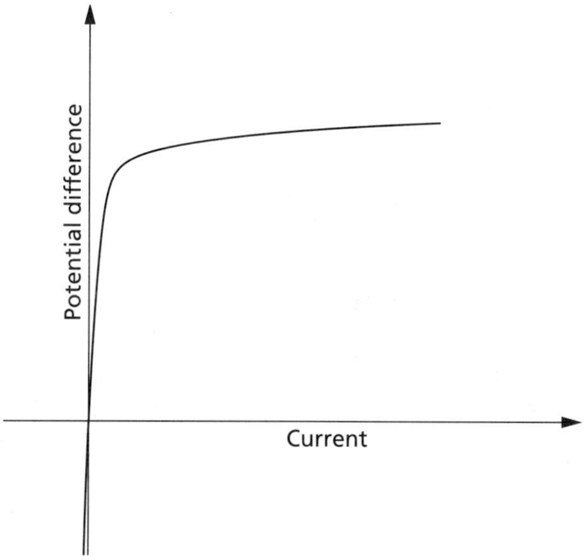

p.d. against current for a semiconductor diode

For a semiconductor diode, as you can see, the current is zero when the voltage is negative, but when it is positive, the current increases sharply. This is involved with its use as a rectifier (see topic seven).

The resistance of most **thermistors** decreases with temperature. Thus they are non-ohmic.

(You are often expected to read off values from graphs in exam questions. This is easy, but a question on resistance may also be included, especially with graphs like those above. You are required to use the formula $V = IR$ to work out what the resistance is at a given voltage or current. Our graphs are drawn as voltage against current. This means that the gradient is the resistance. In the exam, the graph might be drawn as current against voltage. That means that the curves will bend the opposite way to how they do on our graphs. That also means that if you are asked to find the resistance, you will have to realise that it is 1/gradient. If you remember that $R = V/I$, then $I/V = 1/R$, you will be OK.)

Resistance of a wire

As a wire gets longer, it is more difficult for electrons to get all the way through it, so the resistance increases.

Resistance $\propto$ length

The little squiggle, $\propto$, means 'is proportional to', so if the length is doubled, R is doubled.

If the area of the wire increases, and the wire gets thicker, then there is more space for electrons to find their way along the wire, so the resistance decreases.

$$\text{Resistance} \propto \frac{1}{\text{cross-sectional area}}$$

Where something is proportional to 1/something else, it is called **inversely proportional**.

Remember that if the diameter goes up by a factor of three, then the area goes up by a factor of nine as the area is a squared quantity, and so the resistance goes down by a factor of nine.

Total resistance of resistors

In series, the total resistance

$R_T = R_1 + R_2 + R_3 + \ldots$

The powers that be (in their infinite wisdom) have deemed the following section unimportant and thus not in the syllabus. All they want you to realise is that the total resistance of resistors connected in parallel is less than that of the same resistors connected in series.

Total series resistance

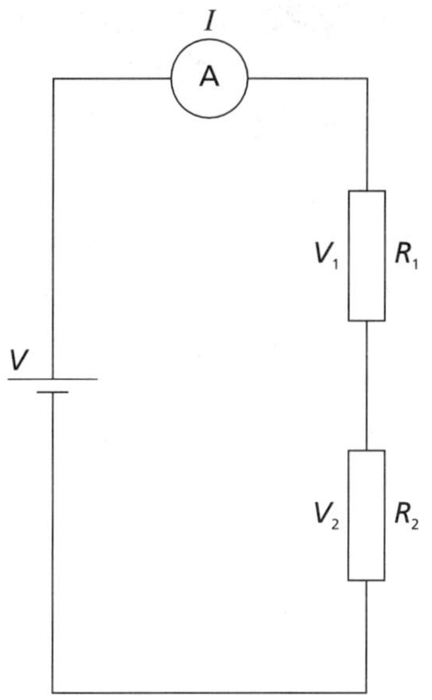

The resistance of the whole circuit is called R_T, and there are two resistors, R_1 and R_2, in series. The current, I, is the same at all points in the circuit. The p.d. across the whole circuit is V.

The p.d. across R_1 plus the p.d. across R_2 is the p.d. across the whole circuit, i.e.

$$V = V_1 + V_2$$

If the total resistance is R_T then:

$$V = IR_T$$

and $V_1 = IR_1$ and $V_2 = IR_2$

$$IR_T = IR_1 + IR_2$$

Dividing by I, we get:

$$R_T = R_1 + R_2$$

It isn't necessary to know the derivation above but it is useful to know how the formula comes about.

Total resistance of parallel resistors

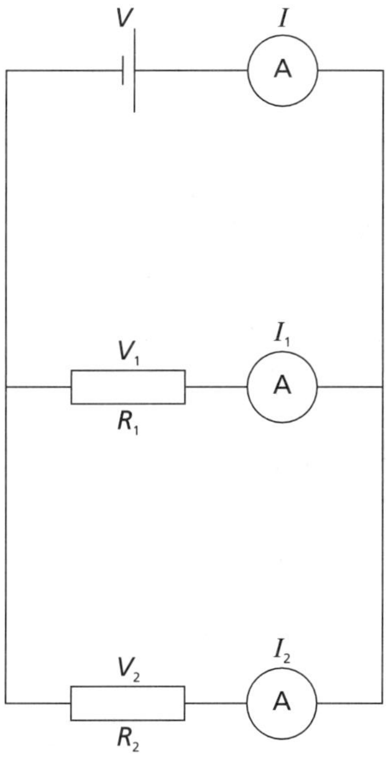

Kirchhoff's first law says that the sum of the currents flowing into a junction is equal to the sum of the currents flowing out. This means that:

$$I = I_1 + I_2$$

If R_T is the total resistance of the parallel resistors, then $V = IR_T$ and:

$$I = \frac{V}{R_T}$$

However

$$I_1 = \frac{V_1}{R_1} \text{ and } I_2 = \frac{V_2}{R_2}$$

Remembering that $V = V_1 = V_2$, because each loop has the same p.d. across it:

$$\frac{V}{R_T} = \frac{V}{R_1} + \frac{V}{R_2}$$

Dividing by V, we get:

$$\frac{1}{R_T} = \frac{1}{R_1} + \frac{1}{R_2}$$

Remember that this gives you $1/R_T$, so you rearrange at the end to find R_T.

Cells in circuits

A **cell** is the part of a circuit that provides the electrical energy, by converting other forms of energy into it. For example, a dry cell undergoes a chemical reaction inside, and converts energy from chemical to electrical. Many cells connected together are called a **battery**.

(Components and wires in a circuit are not the only parts of the circuit that have resistance: the cell has some resistance as well, called ***internal resistance****. Not all the energy that the cell converts to electrical energy is available for the rest of the circuit to convert to other forms. Some of the energy is used up by the cell itself, overcoming its own resistance. In calculations at GCSE, it is usual to ignore this internal resistance.)*

Power and energy

Power the rate of doing work

The power in a circuit is the energy converted per second. It is measured in watts (W).

Power = voltage × current

$$P = VI$$

P power (W)
V voltage (V)
I current (A)

(1 ampere is 1 coulomb per second
1 volt is 1 joule per coulomb

$$\text{volts} \times \text{amperes} = \frac{\text{joules}}{\text{coulombs}} \times \frac{\text{coulombs}}{\text{seconds}} = \frac{\text{joules}}{\text{seconds}}$$

Please, please, please, please, please don't write that in an exam! It's just to explain where we get the power equation from, and to prove that 90% of physics wasn't made up on the spot, as so many misled souls seem to think.)

As power (P) = VI, and $V = IR$, we can say:

$VI = IR \times I = I^2R$

So, electrical power (P) in watts (W):

$$P = VI = I^2R = \frac{V^2}{R}$$

P power (W)
V p.d. (V)
I current (A)
R resistance (Ω)

These rearrangements, though not in the GCSE syllabus, are useful for calculating power when any two of I, V and R are known.

Energy

Energy (W) is power multiplied by time (t), so:

Energy = power × time

$$W = ItV$$

W	energy (J)
I	current (A)
t	time (s)
V	p.d. (V)

For household energy use, energy is measured in kilowatt hours (kilowatts, that is 1000 watts, multiplied by hours). A kilowatt is a unit of power and an hour is a unit of time (3600 seconds), so kilowatt hours are a measure of energy (power multiplied by time). 1 kWh is equivalent to 1 unit of electricity, which costs about 8 p.

1 kilowatt hour (1 kWh) the energy converted by an appliance running at 1 kW, in 1 hour

The cost of electricity is the energy in kWh multiplied by the cost per unit.

(Note that in exam questions, examiners often test your understanding, by using non-SI units which, when used with the equations, will not give the right answer. Always make sure that values have been converted to the right units before calculating your answer.)

Mains electricity

The standard voltage used nowadays is 230 V (a.c. 50 Hz). The mains is a source of alternating p.d., with each cycle of voltage being repeated 50 times per second. (This is why a ticker timer vibrates at 50 times per second.) However, power cables have a much higher voltage, in order to reduce current, and therefore reduce power loss through dissipation of heat. (This is explained in more detail at the end of topic six, electromagnetic induction.)

The plug in this diagram is correctly wired.

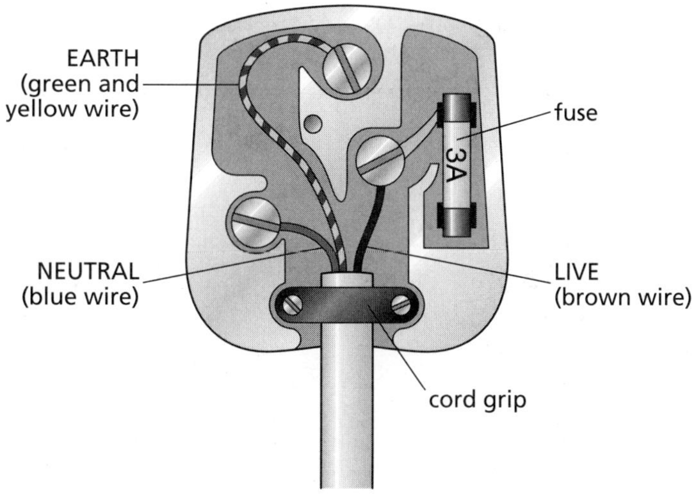

The **live** wire is brown, and is wired to the fuse.
The **neutral** wire is blue and is wired to the terminal on the left-hand side of the plug as viewed from the back.
The **earth** wire is green and yellow, and wired to the terminal connected to the longer pin.
The cord grip prevents stress on the connections in a plug. If a plug is wired for the first time it should be checked before use by someone who knows what they are doing. (These people are few and far between, so it could be useful to make friends with your physics teacher...well, maybe.)

If an appliance has a metallic casing, then the casing may become **live** (it may have a high voltage). It is important that safety precautions are taken. The casing is earthed, so that if it becomes live, the current can flow down the earth wire of the household's ring main, which is itself earthed at the fuse board by a connection to the neutral wire of the supply cable. In older systems a connection to underground piping may be used. In this situation, a large current will flow through the live wire, so that the fuse melts, and breaks the circuit, thus disconnecting the live wire. The fuse should always appear in the live wire part of the circuit.

In exam questions you may well be asked to calculate the optimum value of a fuse. In this case, you should calculate the normal current that would flow through the circuit. The value of the fuse should certainly not be lower than this (or it would blow) so the value you require is the closest value that is higher than your answer. For example, if you calculated the current as being 9 A, then you want a 10 A fuse, rather than a 13 A fuse.

Double insulation
Some appliances have double insulation. These have the symbol ⧈ somewhere on them. Double insulation means that as well as the wires being insulated, the appliance itself has a casing made out of an insulating material; usually plastic. Electric shavers are a good example. There is no chance of the casing becoming live, so it is not usually necessary to wire up to the earth terminal. (But you still need the pin, or the plug doesn't fit in the socket!)

Worked Questions

1. *What happens to the resistance of a lamp as the current increases, and why?*

[3]

Resistance increases, as the increase in current causes an increase in the temperature of the filament [this is the crucial point] and so the particles in the filament are vibrating more, and electrons find it more difficult to move through the wire.

2. *Identify three mistakes in the wiring of the plug below:* [3]

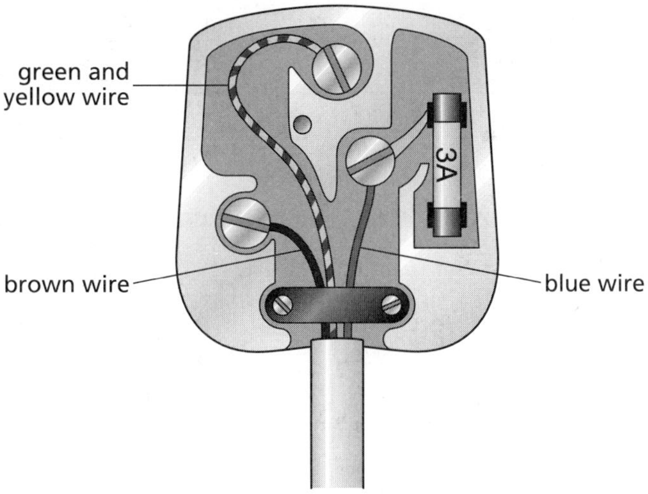

The blue wire is connected to the live terminal.
The brown wire is connected to the neutral terminal.
The cable insulation has been cut back too far, and the cable is not being clenched by the cord grip, so that strain falls on the coloured wires.

3. *What does the symbol ⧈ mean on an electrical appliance?* [2]

It means the appliance is 'double insulated' and does not require an earth connection.

If you hadn't seen the mark allocation for the question, you might have been forgiven for only answering the first half. Use the mark allocation as a guideline. You have to write two separate things to get two marks.

4. *A hair-drier has the following label on it: 230 V 50 Hz 1200 W. Taking the maximum voltage to be 230 V, as given on the label, calculate the maximum current, and suggest a value for the fuse to be installed.* [3]

$P = VI$

Dividing both sides by V to rearrange the formula to:

$$I = \frac{P}{V}$$

$$I = \frac{1200}{230}\ \text{A}$$

$I = 5.2$ A

The fuse should be a 13 A fuse

Even though this is a relatively simple question, be sure to write down all the stages of your working. It's easy once you have learnt something to assume that everyone else will know what you mean with sketchy working.

topic five

electricity and magnetism

Magnets

Magnets are made up of groups of atoms called **domains**, which behave like magnets within magnets.

All magnets have two poles: a '**north-seeking**' or '**N**' pole, and a '**south-seeking**' or '**S**' pole. When a magnet that is allowed to move freely, for instance by being suspended, it always comes to rest so that the north-seeking (N) pole points towards the northern end of the Earth and the south-seeking (S) pole points to the southern end of the Earth.

A freely moving magnet comes to rest in a north–south direction.

A good way to remember this is to bear in mind that a compass, which is just a magnet anyway, always points north.

Like poles repel each other (N and N or S and S), unlike poles attract each other (N and S).

> *(We might think of the Earth itself as an enormous magnet. The north-seeking (N) pole of a bar magnet points roughly towards the Earth's geographical North Pole in the Arctic. However, as unlike poles attract, this must be the Earth's S pole, magnetically speaking. Similarly, the Earth's geographical South Pole, in the Antarctic, is roughly the N pole of 'magnet' Earth.)*

Magnetic materials and making magnets

A material, such as iron, that is both easy to magnetise, and loses its magnetism easily, is called magnetically **soft**.
So logically, a **hard** magnetic material, such as steel, is difficult to magnetise, but keeps its magnetism for longer.

How to make a magnet

Stroke an unmagnetised material in one direction only, with a magnet. What this does, is to line up each domain, so that they are all 'pointing' in the same direction. In the unmagnetised material, the domains are arranged haphazardly, so there is no overall magnetic effect.

Making an electromagnet
An electromagnet behaves like an ordinary magnet, but it is activated by an electric current. If you pass a current through a wire, it causes a magnetic field (see section below). This effect can be enhanced by winding the wire into a coil, with many loops. The advantage of an electromagnet is quite simply, the ability to turn it on and off.

How to demagnetise a magnet

1. Heating. The heat makes the particles move vigorously (see topic nine) messing up the alignment of the domains. Domains arranged haphazardly have no overall magnetic effect.
2. Use a sledgehammer (not joking). The energy of hitting becomes heat (see above for explanation). In fact sometimes you don't even need to hit the magnet hard. Just letting it fall off a table might do.
3. Put the object in a coil, which has alternating current through it, and slowly reduce the current. The effect of this is to slowly break up the arrangement of the domains, as the current, and therefore the direction of the magnetic field, is constantly changing direction.

Magnetic induction

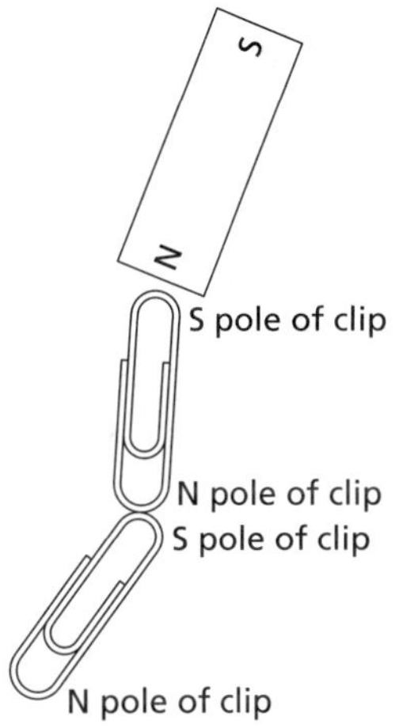

Imagine a paperclip dangling from a magnet. You can get a second one to stick to the first paperclip. Try it if you don't believe me.

The reason for this is that the metal in the paperclip is magnetically soft, that is, easy to magnetise. When it is held close to another magnet (it does not necessarily have to touch it) then magnetism is induced into the paperclip, and it becomes a magnet. However, when you take away the proper magnet, the paperclip loses its magnetism, as soft magnetic materials are easy to demagnetise as well.

Magnetic fields

Magnetic field the area where magnetism acts

The magnetic field is represented by **field lines**. These show the direction of the field. The lines are always labelled with arrows which show the direction in which a plotting compass would point if you placed it in that part of the field, as in the diagram below.

Magnetic field around a bar magnet

The magnetic force is strongest near the poles, where the field lines are closest together.

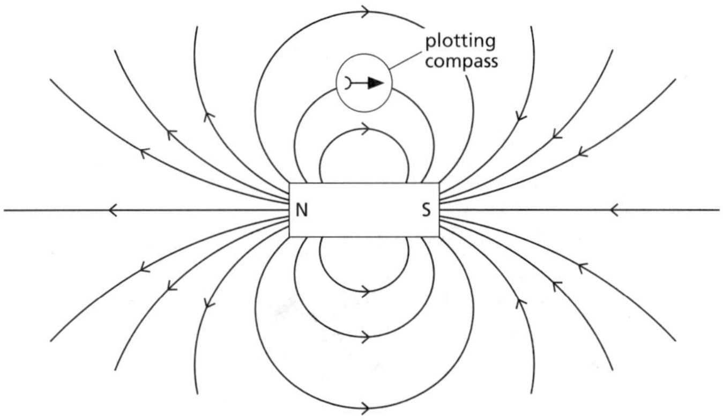

Two bar magnets with unlike poles facing each other

If two magnets are facing each other, N pole to S pole, then they attract each other. The field lines go from the N pole of one magnet to the S pole of the other.

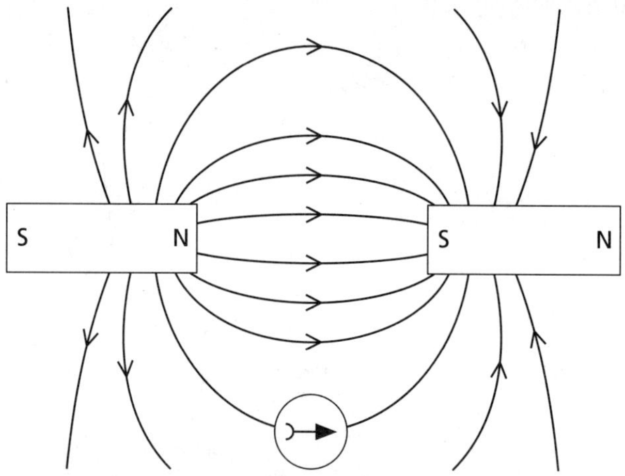

Two bar magnets with like poles facing each other

If two magnets are facing each other, N pole to N pole, and are therefore repelling each other, then there are no field lines between the two N poles. The single point in the centre, in between the two N poles is a **neutral point**.

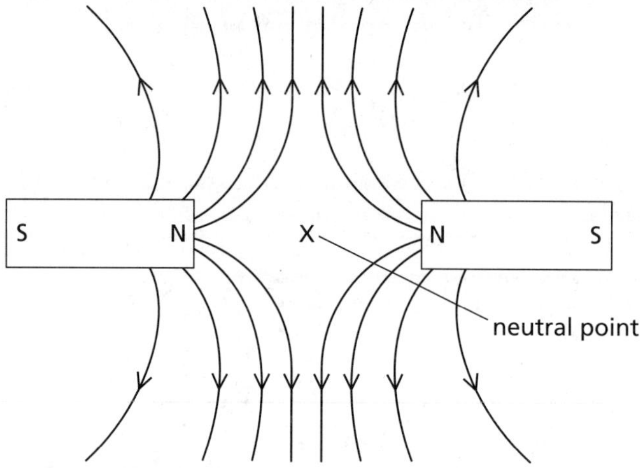

The magnetic effect of a current

A wire carrying a current has a magnetic field around it.

The Right-hand Grip Rule: *If a wire carrying a current is gripped in the right hand, with the thumb pointing in the direction of the conventional current, then the fingers indicate the direction of the magnetic field.*

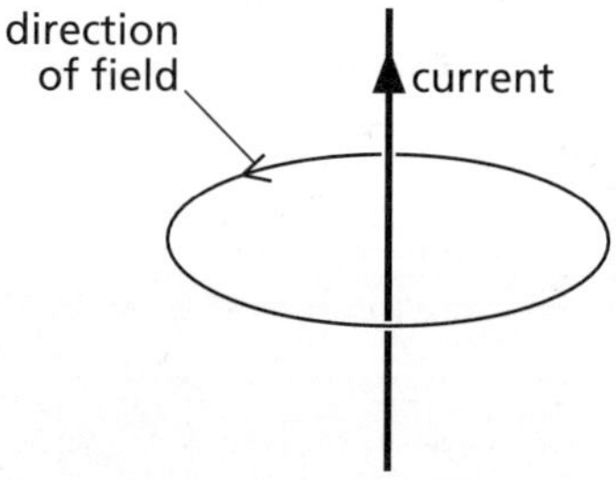

This is one you ought to actually try.

Electromagnets

A **solenoid** is a long coil of wire. When a current is passed through the wire the solenoid has a magnetic field (which is strongest inside the solenoid). A solenoid with a bar of magnetically soft iron, called the **core**, inside it, has a much stronger magnetic field and is called an **electromagnet**.

The shape of the field is the same as the magnetic field around an ordinary bar magnet. The end of the coil that has current flowing anticlockwise round it, as we are facing it, is the N pole, and the end where the current flows clockwise, as we face it, is the S pole. The diagram shows an easy way to remember this.

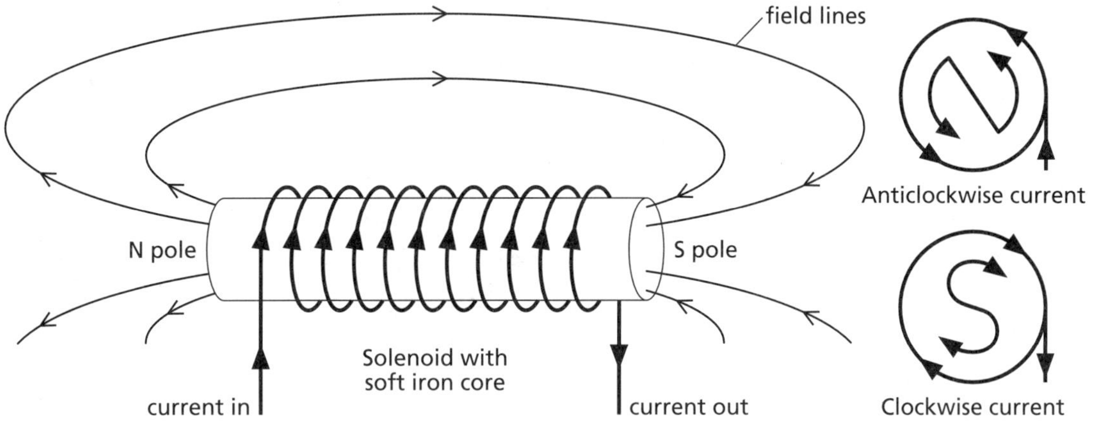

Increasing the strength of the magnetic field of an electromagnet

- Increase the number of turns of wire on the solenoid.
- Increase the size of the current.
- Change the shape of the core, as shown in the diagram. As the poles get closer together, the magnetic field between them gets stronger.

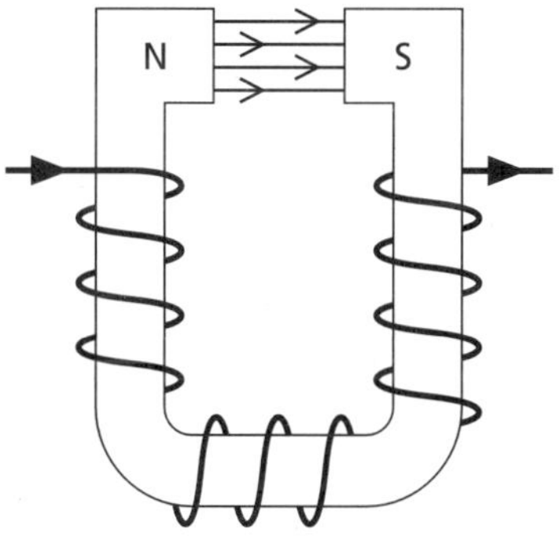

Remember that the electromagnet also has a much stronger magnetic field because of the soft iron core inside the solenoid.

Uses of electromagnets

The advantage of electromagnets is that you can switch them on and off, but they require energy in the form of electricity in order to work.

However, they are very useful and very common. They're in cranes, doorbells, and telephone earpieces. If you get a small metal splinter in your eye, and go to hospital, it is likely that it will be removed using an electromagnet. They are also used in hospitals for magnetic resonance imaging (MRI).

The motor effect

If a wire carrying a current is placed in a magnetic field, at right angles to the direction of the field, it experiences a force. This force is at right angles to the direction of the current and the direction of the magnetic field. This is called the **motor effect**.

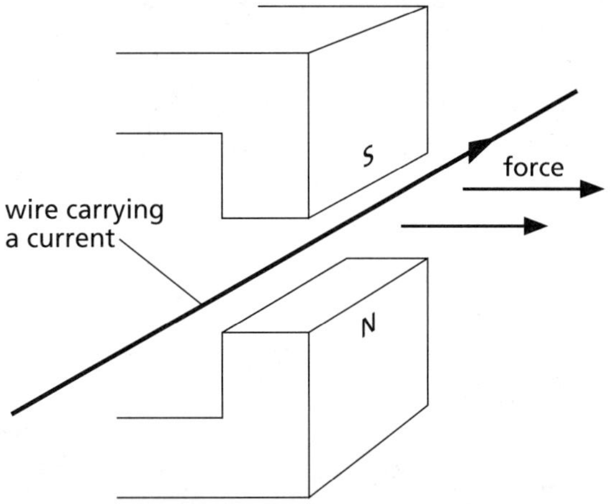

The wire would be catapulted sideways, as shown (if it were free to move!)

This happens because the magnetic field created by the current in the wire interacts with the field from the magnet.

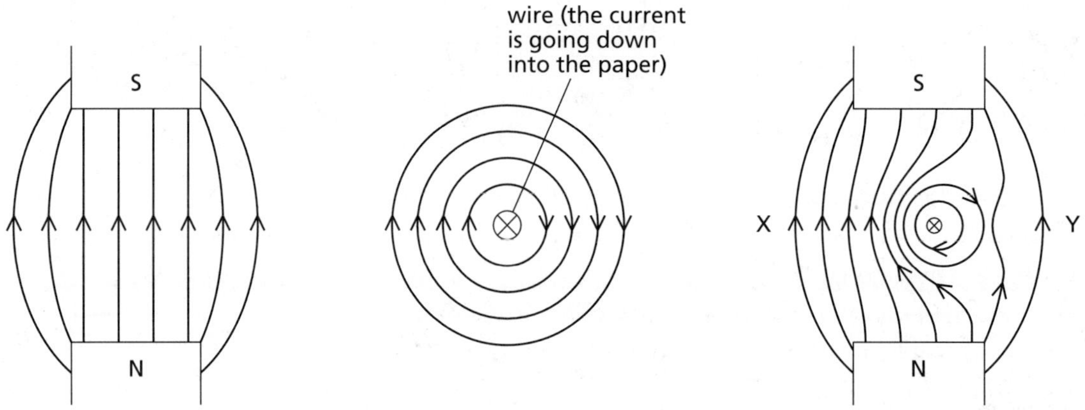

Magnetic field of the magnet | Magnetic field created by the current | Combined field of magnet and current

The combined field at side X is very strong, as both fields are acting in the same direction, but on side Y the combined field is weak as the two fields are acting in opposite directions. The force acts towards the weak side. You can imagine the field lines as stretched rubber bands which would catapult the wire sideways.

Fleming's Left-hand Rule for the Motor Effect: *If the thumb, the first finger, and the second finger of the left hand are held at right angles to each other, then:*

The ***F****irst finger points in the direction of the* ***F****ield (N to S)*

*The se****C****ond finger points in the direction of the* ***C****urrent*

*The thu****M****b points in the direction of the* ***M****otion of the wire.*

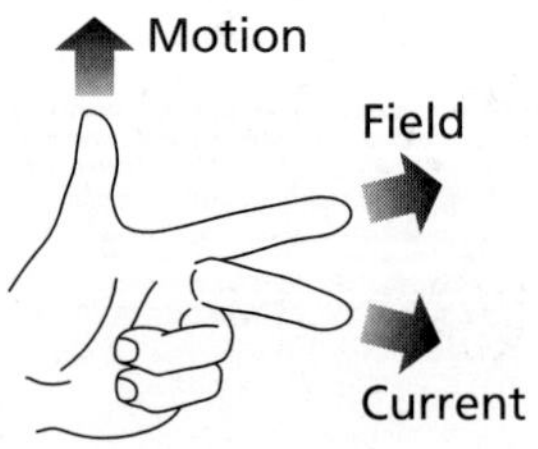

The direct current (d.c.) motor

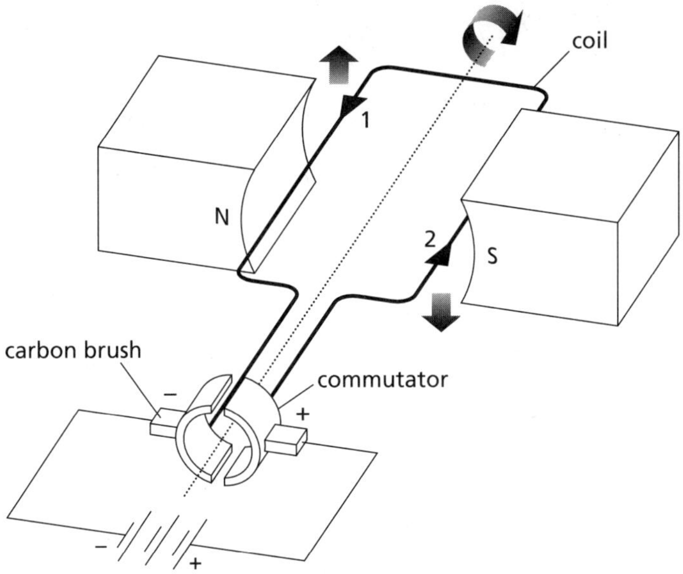

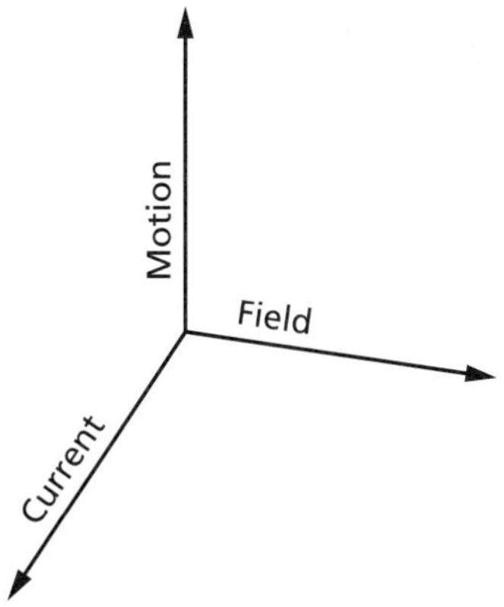

In the d.c. motor shown in the diagram, current enters and leaves the coil through the **split-ring commutator**. (The carbon brushes are in contact with the commutator, allowing current to flow whilst it is rotating.)

The current is flowing towards you in wire 1, and away from you in wire 2. According to the Left-hand Rule, the force on wire 1 acts upwards and the force on wire 2 acts downwards. The coil and commutator turn clockwise. When the coil is at 90° to the field, the gaps in the commutator are next to the carbon brushes, so there is no current. However, the momentum of the coil keeps it moving round. The connections to the commutator are now reversed, so that the direction of the current in the coil is also reversed: current is flowing into wire 1, and out of wire 2, so the motion is still clockwise.

This is a simple direct current motor. It does not have a steady rotation, as the **torque** (moment) is changing continually, going from a maximum to zero (when there is a gap in the commutator). If there were more turns on the coil, it would be more powerful, and the motion could be made smoother by winding many coils around a soft iron core at different angles. In a modern d.c. motor, the magnet is more likely to be an electromagnet.

Galvanometer an instrument that will detect an electric current

A moving-coil galvanometer is, as its name implies, an instrument that has a coil between the poles of a magnet; the coil moves when a current is passed through it, which turns a pointer.

Worked Questions

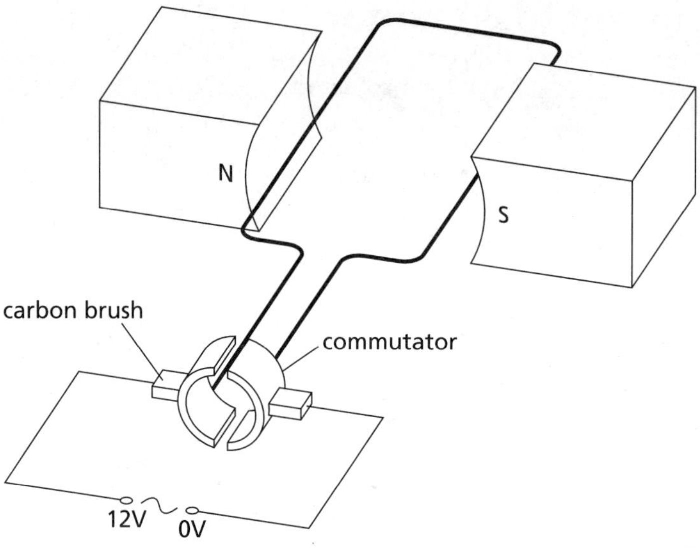

1. *Why does the motor not work properly?* [2]

The diagram shows a d.c. (direct current) motor, and, as you might expect, it only works with a d.c. power supply. In the diagram it is connected to an a.c. (alternating current) power supply. Words to this effect might get you only one mark, however, so it's necessary to give more information if you want that A*. The answer which receives full marks is:

> This type of motor (d.c.) can only work when current flows in one direction.* By connecting it to an a.c. supply, the direction of current in the circuit is constantly reversing, causing the motor to reverse its direction constantly.*

The circuit is now connected to a d.c. power supply.

2. *Suggest two ways of making the motor turn faster.* [2]

With these types of question, there are almost always more than two alternatives which will get you marks. In this case there are four possible answers, any two of which will get you full marks for the question.

- Use a stronger magnet.
- Use more turns on the coil.
- Increase the current in the coil.
- Use more coils at differing angles.

3. *Apart from changing the direction of the current, how could you reverse the motion of the coil?* [1]

This is an example of the 'easy one-marker' in an exam question that has many parts. It is similar to the previous question but instead targets one particular answer. If you know it, it's easy, but if you don't, you'll have to think in terms of Fleming's Left-hand Rule (motor effect) and see for yourself that you only need to reverse one of the directions to change the motion of the coil.

> Swap the magnet's poles around.

A bar magnet is placed on a cork, floating on water, in such a way, that it is free to move in a horizontal plane. It is in a dish which is on a flat table.

4. *In what position will the magnet come to rest?* [1]

This question you will simply have to learn the facts for. Just remember that a compass points north.

The N pole will point towards the north, the S pole towards the south.

A small plotting compass is brought near to one of the poles of the magnet. The plotting compass points towards that pole of the magnet.

5. *Does this end of the magnet point towards polar bears? (That is, does it point towards the North Pole of the Earth, or the South Pole?) How did you come to your answer?* [4]

This is about as hard as GCSE questions get. Don't take too much comfort from that because you will have to understand these harder questions to earn your A*. It is a good idea to go through in your mind, all you have learnt about magnets. Hopefully you will pick out certain facts, for instance, that a plotting compass points along the field lines.

A plotting compass needle points along the field lines.* Field lines go from the N pole of a magnet, to the S pole.* So if the needle points towards a pole, then as the field lines are going from N to S, that pole is the S pole. The N pole of a magnet is north-seeking,* so the S (south-seeking) pole of a magnet points towards the South Pole of the Earth. As polar bears are not found at the South Pole, the end of the magnet that the plotting compass points to does not point towards polar bears.* P.S. Don't worry if you didn't know about polar bears. Your exam paper will not ask you in this particular style.

* Shows where individual marks are awarded in multiple mark questions. You see it can sometimes pay to write what you know even when you aren't sure of the answer. Don't try this too often though; Sod's Law says it will backfire. (Sod's Law: If it can go wrong, it will.)

topic six

electromagnetic induction

The dynamo or generator effect

Imagine you have a circuit, that does not contain a cell. You then take the wire, and move it through a magnetic field so that it cuts across the field lines. A **voltage is induced**. If the circuit is a complete one, then a **current** is also induced. This is **electromagnetic induction**.

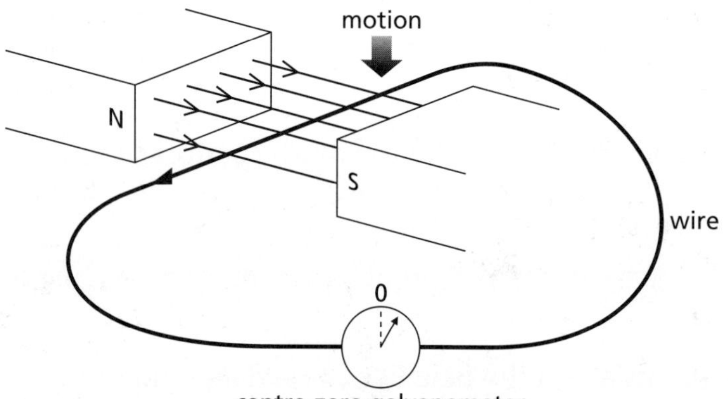

How is the current induced? The changing magnetic field causes the electrons to start moving. Either the field or the wire could be moving; it is the motion of the wire and the field relative to each other that is important.

The size of the induced voltage

The induced voltage, and therefore the induced current in a circuit, increases if:

- The magnetic field strength is greater (which means the magnetic field lines are closer together).
- The wire moves faster across the magnetic field lines.

Putting these two together, we get:

Faraday's Law: *The voltage induced is proportional to the rate at which the wire cuts magnetic field lines.*

The direction of the induced current

Fleming's Right-hand Rule, for the Dynamo Effect: *If the thumb, the first finger, and the second finger of the right hand are held at right angles to each other, then:*

The ***F****irst finger points in the direction of the* ***F****ield (N toS)*

*The se****C****ond finger points in the direction of conventional* ***C****urrent (+ve to –ve)*

*The thu****M****b points in the direction of the* ***M****otion of the conductor.*

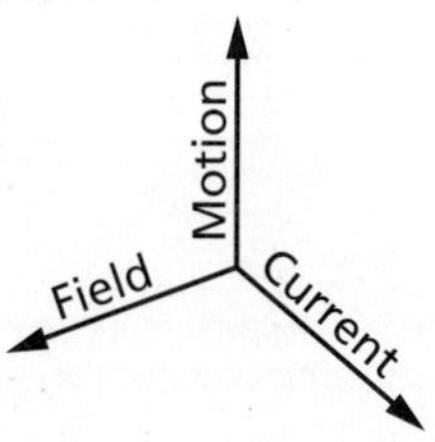

(How do you remember which is which? Dynamo effect or motor effect, Left-hand Rule or Right-hand Rule? Well, you use the mnemonic: ***Motors*** *drive on the* ***Left-hand*** *side of the road – in the UK, at any rate!)*

A voltage can be induced by dipping a magnet in and out of a coil. As the magnet in the diagram below is moved into the coil, the coil cuts field lines all around the magnet, and a current is induced in the direction shown. (Remember the field is all around the magnet, not just in the plane of the page). You could say that dipping the magnet in increases the magnetic field inside the coil, and the changing magnetic field induces the current in one direction. Taking the magnet out causes the magnetic field in the coil to decrease, and a current is induced in the opposite direction.

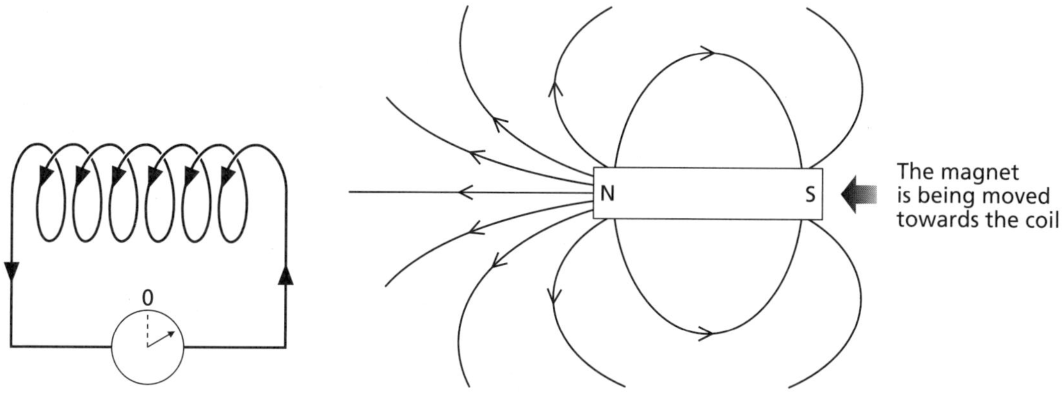

(If you want to try applying Fleming's Right-hand Rule to the situation shown in the diagram above (you wouldn't be asked for this in a GCSE exam), remember that the thumb points in the direction of motion of the conductor. *Here the coil isn't moving and the magnet is being moved from right to left. So the relative motion of the conductor is from left to right, and that is the direction in which to point your thumb.)*

As the N pole of the magnet is brought near the coil, that end of the coil becomes an N pole, and tries to repel the magnet. As the N pole is brought out, that end of the coil becomes a S pole to oppose the motion of the magnet and attract it back in.

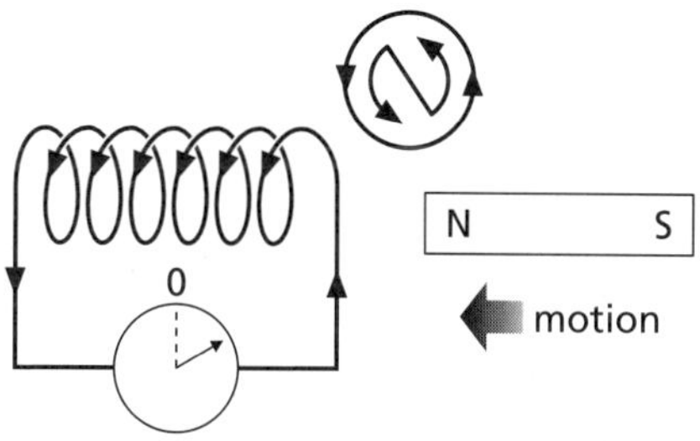

Look again at the wire being moved *downwards* through a magnetic field (diagram on page 64). Because of the dynamo effect the wire is now carrying a current. The wire is still in a magnetic field. As stated in topic five, a current flowing in a magnetic field brings about the motor effect. If you apply Fleming's Left-hand Rule for the motor effect, you will see that the direction of the motor effect force is *upwards.*

This means that the conductor experiences a force trying to slow it down. However, the actual force due to the motor effect is quite small. The important thing is that the motion which would be brought about by the motor effect is in the opposite direction to the motion of the wire that was used in the dynamo effect.

Lenz's Law: *The direction of an induced current in a circuit is always such as to oppose the change that caused it.*

This means that if you induce a current in a coil by pushing a magnet through it, this current creates a field opposing the motion of the magnet. You feel a force opposing your pushing the magnet into the coil. If you think about it, this has to happen, otherwise you would be getting the current without using energy.

A dynamo on a bicycle

A magnet on the wheel rotates near a coil. The field lines are cut by the wire of the coil. The magnet keeps rotating, as you pedal, and the field lines keep getting cut. The current induced is enough to light a lamp.

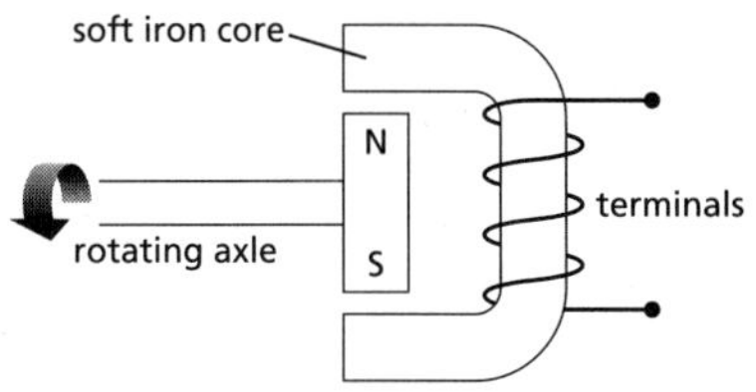

A simple alternating current (a.c.) generator

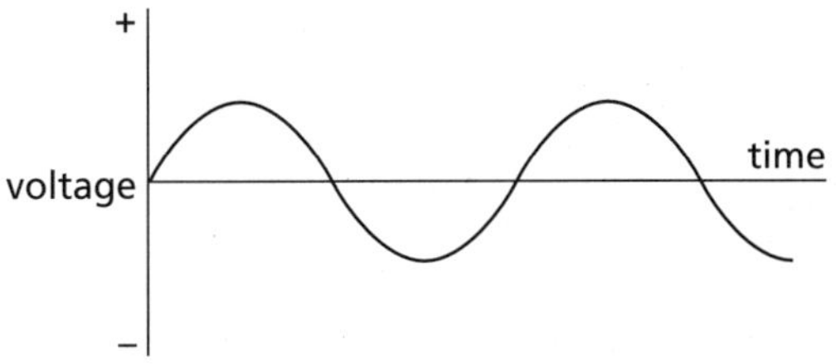

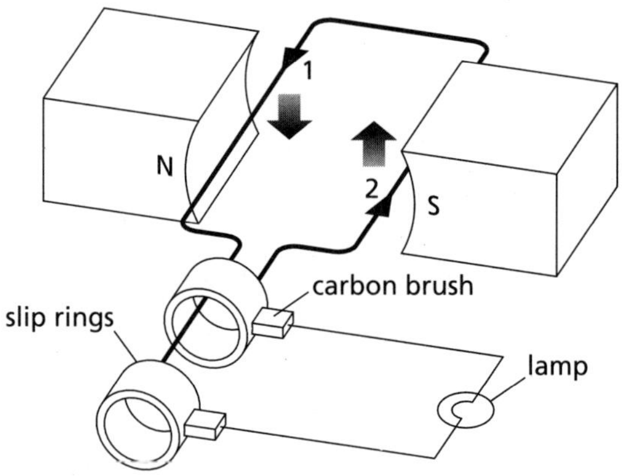

The slip rings (not commutators, they have no gap) are connected to carbon brushes. The reason they are there is so that the wire does not get tangled when it rotates. If wire 1 is moved downwards, then, from Fleming's Right-hand Rule, current flows out of wire 1 and current flows into wire 2. After half a revolution, wire 1 is now moving upwards, so the current flows out of wire 1 and into wire 2. The current has been reversed, and therefore flows the opposite way through the lamp.

Transformers

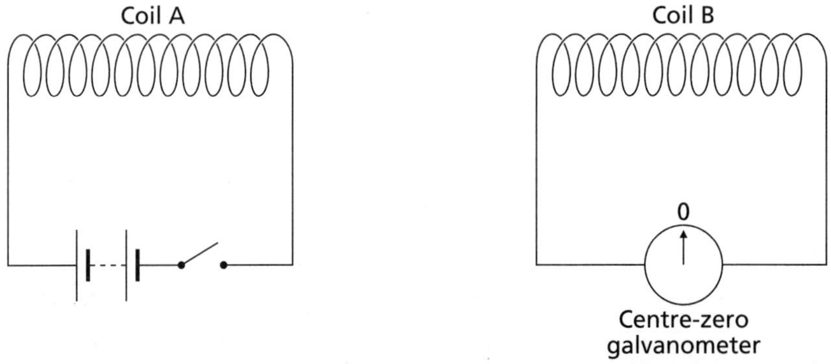

When the circuit in coil A is switched on, it becomes an electromagnet. This produces a magnetic field around coil B. The magnetic field around B changes from zero to high, but only for a moment; it stays high. Current is induced in coil B during the time it takes for the magnetic field to go from zero to high. Note that current is only induced when the magnetic field is changing. If there was a lamp connected to B, it would flash. The needle of the galvanometer (a device which shows the direction of current) flicks one way and then falls back to zero. When coil A is switched off, the magnetic field drops from high to zero. This again, induces a brief current in coil B in the opposite direction, and the galvanometer needle briefly flicks the other way.

*The current is induced by the **changing** magnetic field.*

However your hands would get pretty tired if you had to keep pressing switches on and off. Instead you can supply an alternating current (a.c.) to coil A. As the size and direction of the a.c. are always changing, coil A produces a magnetic field that is continually changing. This in turn induces an alternating voltage in coil B (and an alternating current if coil B is part of a circuit). The strength of the magnetic field, and so the size of the induced voltage, can be made very much greater if the coils are wound around a soft iron core, as shown in the diagram.

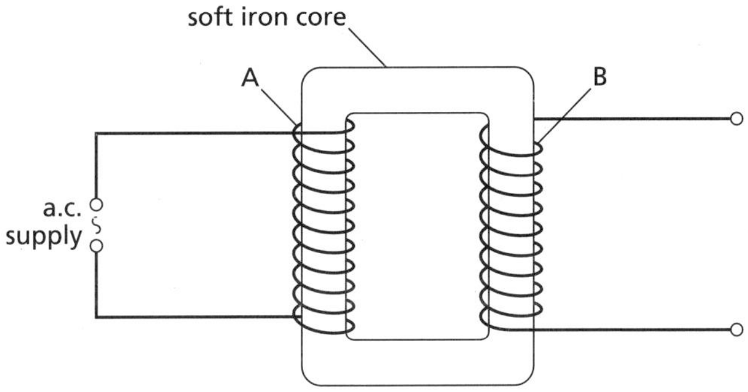

If coil A is connected to an a.c. supply then:

- the arrangement is a **transformer**
- A is called the **primary coil**
- B is called the **secondary coil**.

The transformer equations

$$\frac{\text{Voltage across secondary coil}}{\text{Voltage across primary coil}} = \frac{\text{Number of turns on secondary coil}}{\text{Number of turns on primary coil}}$$

$$\frac{V_s}{V_p} = \frac{n_s}{n_p}$$

V_s voltage across secondary coil
V_p voltage across primary coil
n_s number of turns on secondary coil
n_p number of turns on primary coil

If the transformer were 100% efficient, then:
Input power to primary coil = output power from secondary coil, or

$$V_p I_p = V_s I_s$$

V_p voltage across primary coil
I_p current in primary coil
V_s voltage across secondary coil
I_s current in secondary coil

Note that if the voltage in A, for instance, goes up, the current goes down, because power stays the same.

(We can rearrange the equation $V_pI_p = V_sI_s$ *to* $V_s/V_p = I_p/I_s$*, and therefore:* $n_s/n_p = I_p/I_s$*.)*

If n_s is greater than n_p, the transformer is **step-up**: the voltage in the secondary coil is greater than in the primary if there are more turns on the secondary coil. However, the current in the secondary is less than in the primary.
If n_s is less than n_p, the transformer is **step-down**: the voltage in the secondary coil is less than in the primary if there are fewer turns on the secondary coil, but the current in the secondary is greater than in the primary.

Large transformers can be 99% (or more) efficient. Energy is lost because of induced eddy currents in the core. This can be avoided by making the core out of layers (lamination) and insulating each layer. Using magnetically soft materials reduces the energy lost as the core magnetises and demagnetises.

Uses of transformers:

- To get low voltages from the mains 230 V a.c., e.g. for radios.
- To get high voltages from the mains, e.g. for TV.
- Power packs sometimes offer different voltages. How? They use transformers, of course.
- In the National Grid.

The National Grid system uses high voltages in power cables to save on energy losses. The high voltages are produced using step-up transformers, and at the end of the line, step-down transformers in substations are used to bring the voltage down to 230 V.

If the resistance in the power cables is R, then the power lost is I^2R. As you can see, the lower you can make I the less power you lose. A high current is therefore wasteful, because power loss is higher. Also, a high current heats the cables, which in turn raises the resistance. So transformers are used to produce a very high voltage, and thus a low current. This increases efficiency. The voltage across cables can exceed 132 kV (132 000 V), and sometimes it can be as high as 400 kV.

Worked Questions

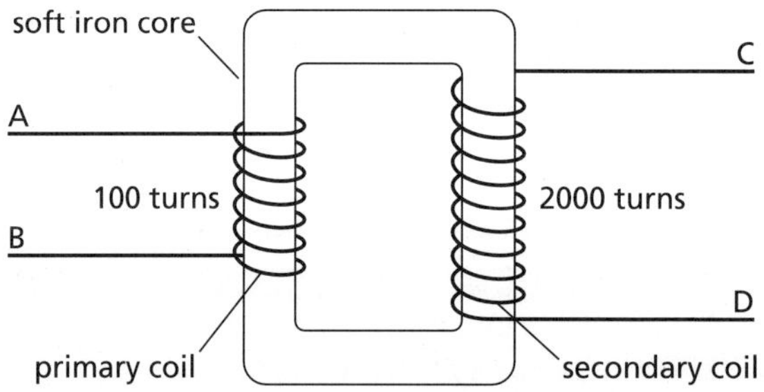

1. *Is this a step-up or step-down transformer? Give a reason.* [2]

   Step up, as there are more turns on the secondary coil.

2. *In which coil will the current be greater, and by how much? (Assume the transformer is 100% efficient.)* [2]

Using: $\frac{n_s}{n_p} = \frac{I_p}{I_s}$ $\frac{n_s}{n_p} = \frac{2000}{100} = 20$

so: $\frac{I_p}{I_s} = 20$

$\Rightarrow I_p = 20\ I_s$

The current is 20 times greater in the primary coil.

3. *Assuming the transformer is 90% efficient, suggest one way of improving the efficiency of the transformer, and explain how it works.* [2]

The core could be made out of many layers, with each layer being separated by insulating material. This helps stop eddy currents flowing in the core.

4. *Suppose that coil CD is now the primary coil, and AB the secondary coil. Assuming that the transformer is 100% efficient, how many extra turns must be put on coil CD for AB to have a power output of 2300 W, and have a voltage of 230 V across it, if CD is known to have a current of 0.005 A through it?* [6]

Note that the transformer has been reversed: it is step-down.

The power in AB is 2300 W. That means the power in CD is also 2300 W (the transformer is 100% efficient).*

$P = VI \quad \therefore V = \frac{P}{I}$ * Both sides divided by I

So, the voltage in CD is 2300/0.005 = 460 kV.*
Therefore the ratio, voltage CD : voltage AB is 460 000:230 which is 2000:1.*

Using the transformer equation: $\frac{n_s}{n_p} = \frac{V_s}{V_p}$ *

The ratio, number of turns on coil CD : number of turns on coil AB is 2000:1.*

As there are 100 turns on coil AB, there should therefore now be:
$100 \times 2000 = 200\ 000$ turns on coil CD.*

There are already 2000 turns on CD, so it needs
200 000 – 2000 = 198 000 more turns.*

You can see that there is more than one way of getting the allotted six marks. Don't shoot yourself in the foot by leaving out working. Even a correct final answer without working gets only one mark. If your final answer is wrong, you don't want to lose any more through laziness.

topic seven

electronics

Important components

Variable resistors

These have the symbol:

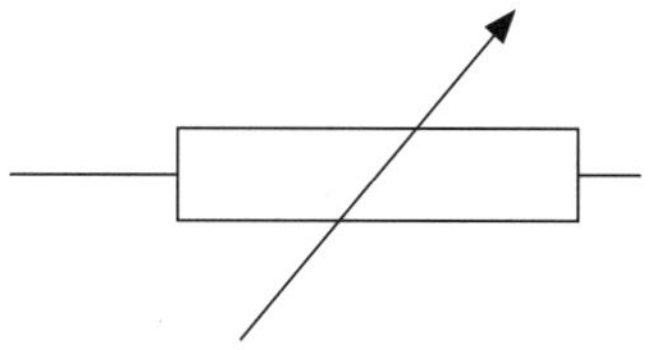

You can adjust a variable resistor to get the resistance you need.

A **rheostat** is a variable resistor, which can be made of metal wire, or carbon. Often, it is a coil of wire with a carbon brush that you can slide along it. This varies the length of the coil, and so also varies its resistance.

A **potentiometer** is a special type of rheostat.

Potentiometers

The potentiometer has three terminals. The terminal with the arrowhead represents the carbon brush that you can slide along the coil.

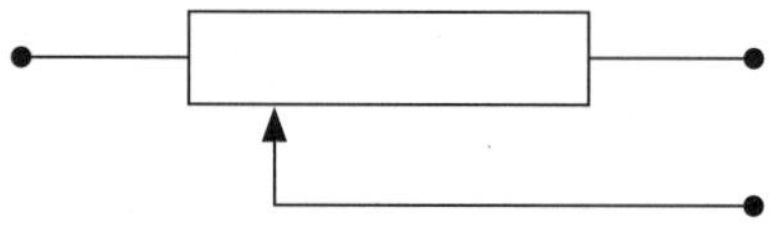

If the third terminal is connected as shown below, then the component is being used as a variable resistor.

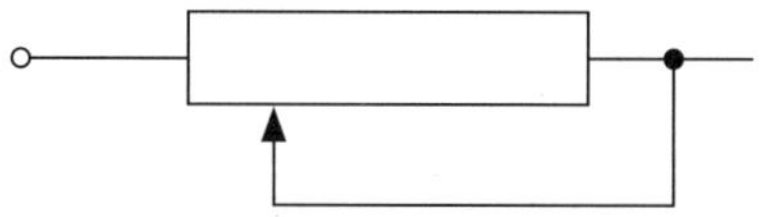

More importantly, it can also be used as a **potential divider**.

The potentiometer coil can be seen as two resistors in series: one represents the part of the coil on one side of the brush, and the second represents the part of the coil on the other side of the carbon brush.

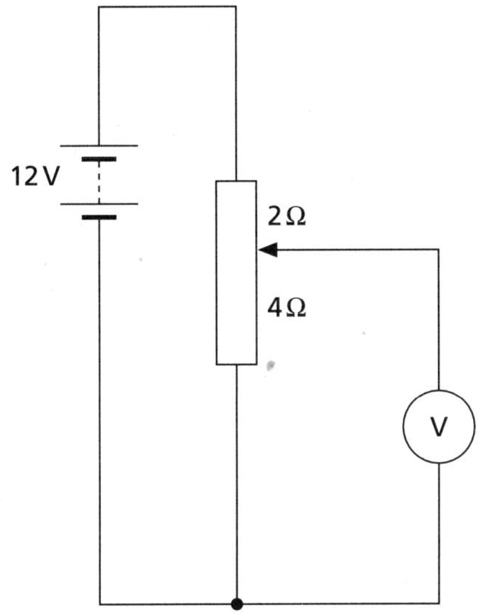

This circuit is essentially the same as the one shown above.

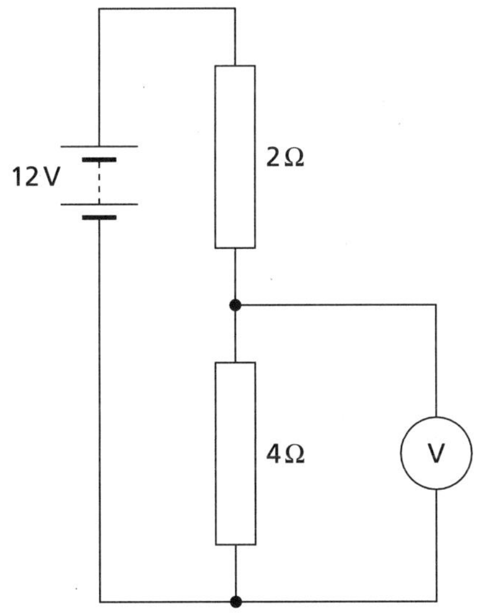

The total resistance is 6 Ω.
Both the resistors carry the same current.
4 Ω is ⅔ of the total resistance.
Therefore, it has ⅔ of the voltage across it.

$$V = \tfrac{2}{3} \times 12\ \text{V}$$
$$= 8\ \text{V}$$

The voltage across the resistor marked 4 Ω is 8 V.

You can see that the voltmeter in both circuits should read 8 V. It is connected across a resistor that has two-thirds of the total resistance, so the resistor has two-thirds of the total voltage across it, that is, 8 V.

Generalising (so that we can get some kind of formula to work out all similar cases):

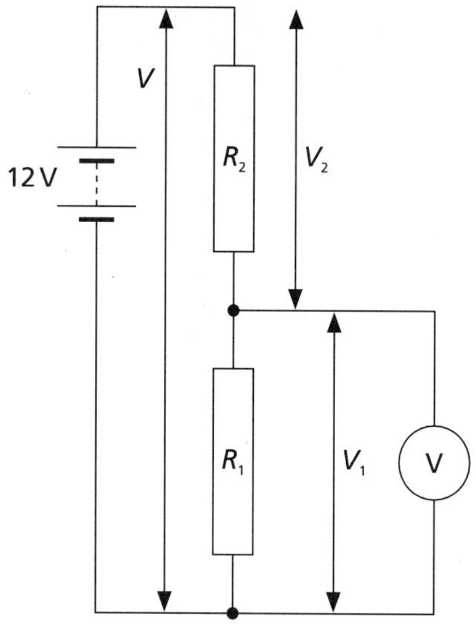

The bit of the potentiometer that has the higher resistance has a higher voltage across it. This comes from Ohm's Law; the current is constant in a series circuit, so the higher the resistance, the higher the potential difference (p.d.) across it. Therefore, the voltmeter in the diagram would give a higher reading if the resistance of the resistor was higher.

The potential divider equation (with reference to the diagram above), is:

$$V_1 = \left(\frac{R_1}{R_1 + R_2}\right) \times V$$

It is just simple proportion when you think what the equation actually means (although, for simple proportion to hold, both the resistors must carry the same current).

However, another important assumption has to be made: the equation only works if the current drawn off (by the voltmeter, in the case above) is very small. Voltmeters tend not to draw too much current, but components like lamps draw appreciable current.

Diodes

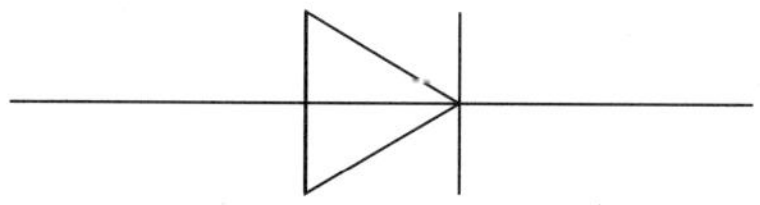

These are made of two types of **semiconductor** material. These are materials that are difficult to classify as either metals or non-metals. A common example is silicon, a less common one is germanium. Semiconductors are 'doped' with impurities. One type of impurity gives **n-type** doping, the other **p-type** doping. A junction between an n-type material and a p-type material is called a **p–n junction**. Diodes are p–n junctions. P–n junctions are **rectifiers**. This means that current can only flow through the diode in one direction.

Current only flows through the diode if the diode is **forward-biased** (the right way round, with the arrow in the symbol pointing in the direction of conventional current). If the diode is reverse-biased, current is almost zero (see the graphs in topic four – electricity).

Light-emitting diodes (LEDs) imaginative name for certain types of diodes which can emit light

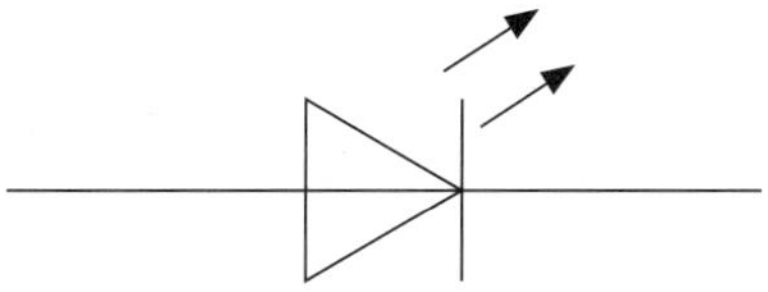

LEDs should only have about 2 V placed across them, so they need a resistor in series with the diode to bring down the p.d. across the diode.

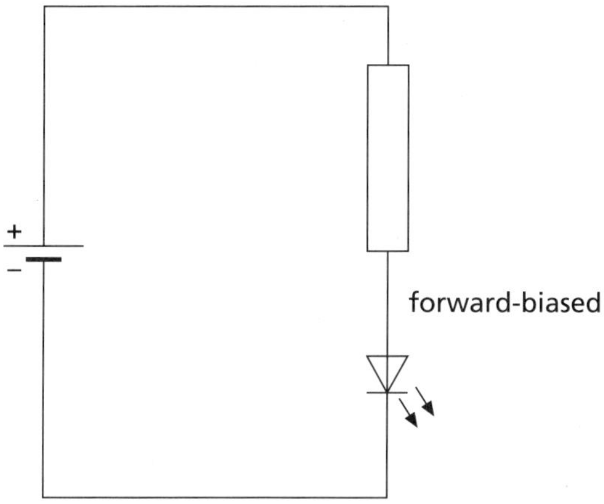

Notice that the diode points in the direction of conventional current (positive to negative)

See the questions at the end of the topic for a calculation of an appropriate resistance.

Capacitors

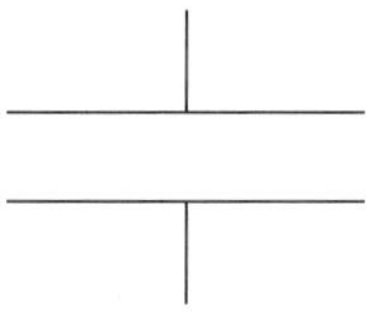

These are just two metal plates with a gap in between, that is filled by an insulator, which could be air, or waxed paper, or a whole host of other things. Capacitors store charge.

Light-dependent resistors (LDR)

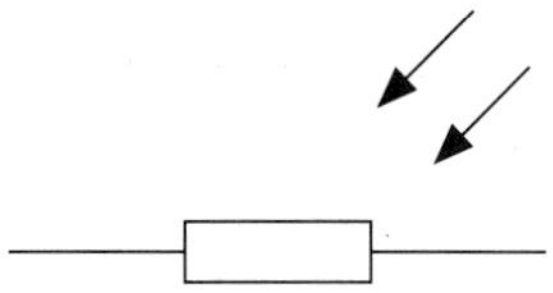

As the intensity of the light shining on the resistor increases, the resistance of the LDR decreases.

Reed switch and relay

Reed switch

This consists of two metal reeds that are normally open. If a magnet is brought close to the switch, it brings the two reeds together and completes the circuit.

Reed relay

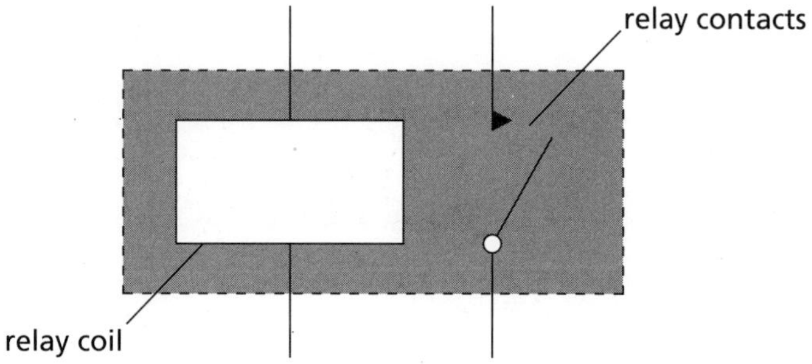

A reed relay is a coil with a reed switch inside it. In the circuit shown below, a small current through the relay produces a magnetic field which switches on the reed switch in the other circuit, so that a larger current can be controlled. The current in the circuit with the coil is quite small, as the resistance of the coil is high.

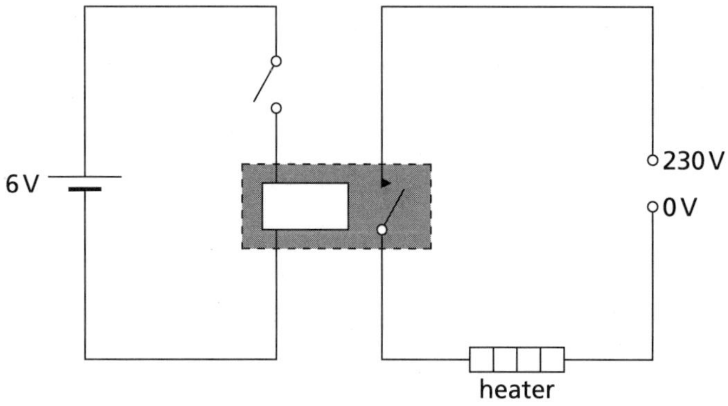

Instead of switching on a separate circuit, the relay could be used to switch on a current in a part of the circuit that was parallel to the coil. Parallel parts of circuits can basically be treated as separate circuits in calculation. (But not quite as much in practice.)

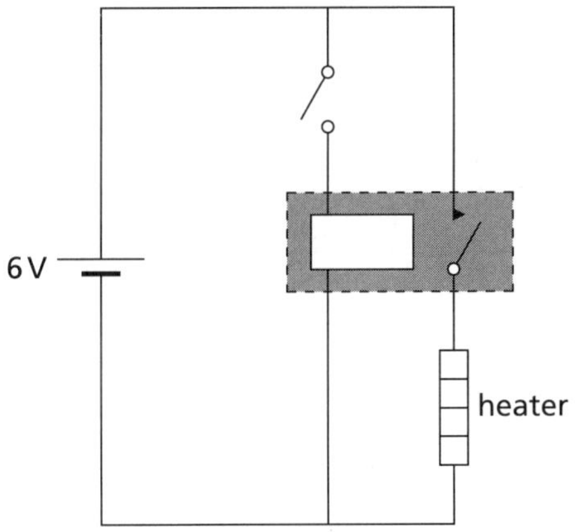

Transistors

The transistor is a **current amplifier**. It is an n-p-n, or p-n-p semiconductor sandwich.

It has three parts to it, as labelled in the diagram: **base, collector** and **emitter**.

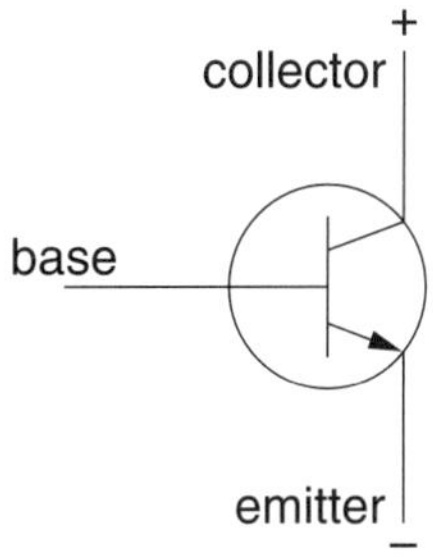

A small change in current in the base circuit produces a large change in current in the collector circuit.

If no current flows in the base circuit, no current flows in the collector circuit.

The diagram shows a transistor being used as a light-dependent switch.

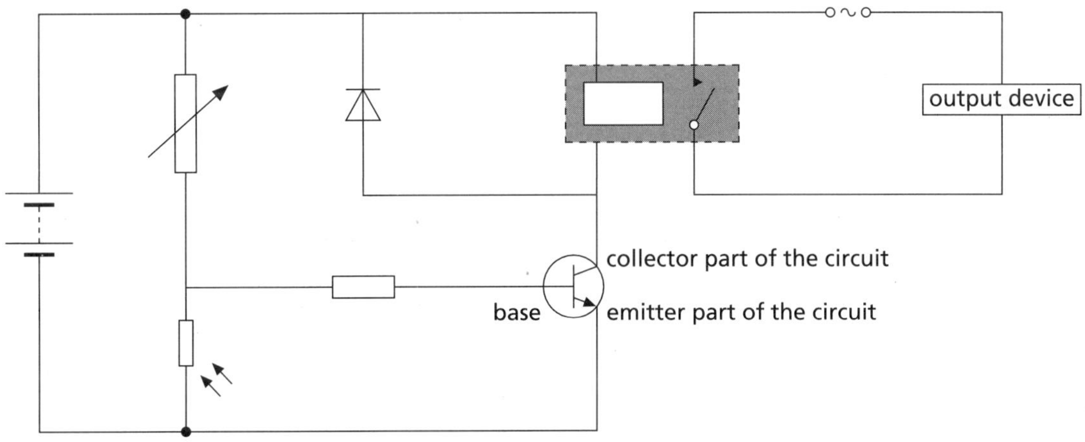

When light is shining on the LDR, its resistance is low. The voltage drop across the LDR is also low, from the potential divider principle. So, a low voltage is applied to the base circuit, which means that no current flows in the collector. The output device is not activated.

When light is not shining, the resistance of the LDR increases. Thus the voltage drop across it increases, and the base voltage is high. This causes a current to flow in the collector, and the relay is activated, and the output device switched on.

When light is not shining on the LDR, the output device is switched on. However, if the LDR and the variable resistor 'swapped places', then the output device would be switched off. Work through the arguments in the previous paragraph, and see if you can figure out why.

Similar circuits are used in street lamps, which automatically switch on when it goes dark.

(The diode is there to protect the transistor. When the transistor switches off the current through the coil, there is a large induced voltage, which could damage the transistor. The diode, which is connected in the reverse direction to the current through the coil and transistor, acts as a short circuit across the coil.)

Transducers

These are electrical components that convert energy, e.g. bulbs, or motors.

Systems

An electronic circuit, as opposed to an electric circuit, is a system. A system responds to the outside world.

The structure of a system:

Input transducers → processors → output transducers

For example for a computer:

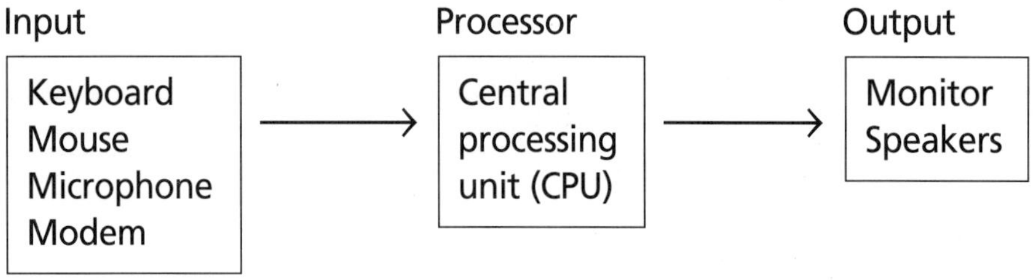

The output from a system may include **feedback**, which is a signal that goes to the input. Useful feedback is always **negative**, i.e. it switches the input off. For instance, a thermostat is a device to keep temperature constant. If the temperature gets too high, the input (the heating) is switched off; if the temperature falls too low, the input is switched back on.

Types of electronic systems

Analogue the voltage can vary smoothly between high and low

Digital voltage is in definite steps, and information is described in digits

A digital system that uses two digits is called **binary** digital: either the voltage is high (near 6 V), which is called **logic 1**, or low (near 0 V), which is called **logic 0**. So the two digits are 1 and 0.

Digital electronics

Logic gates are components that take a logical input, process it, and give a logical output. A certain code of binary input will open the gate, that is, it will give a logic 1 output. There are five types of logic gate: AND, OR, NAND, NOR and NOT, and they are often used in combination. Logic gates require their own power supply.

Truth tables are tables that show the combinations of inputs for logic gates, and the resulting output.

NOT gate (also called an inverter)

A NOT gate has only one input. This can either be 1 or 0. This gate just **inverts** or gives the opposite of its input

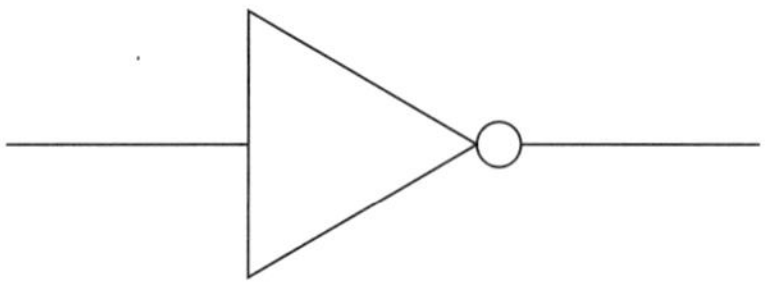

Input	Output
0	1
1	0

A high voltage input (logic 1) gives a low voltage output (logic 0), and vice versa.

AND gate

An AND gate has two inputs, A and B, each of which can only be 1 or 0. This means that an AND gate can have four possible combinations of inputs. The AND gate gives a **logic 1 output only when both A and B are high** (logic 1).

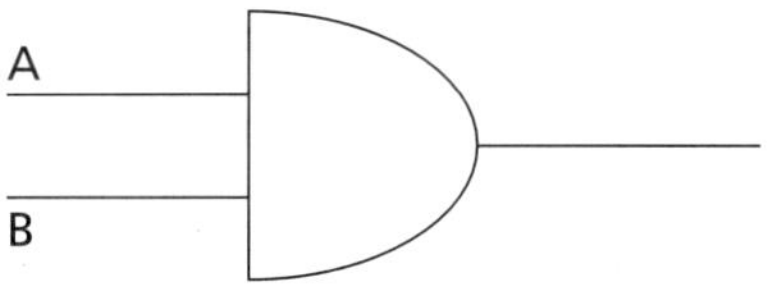

Input A	Input B	Output
0	0	0
0	1	0
1	0	0
1	1	1

Two high inputs give a high output.

OR gate

An OR gate also has two inputs and guess what ... each one can be either 1 or 0. The OR gate gives **output logic 1 when either input A or input B or both are high**.

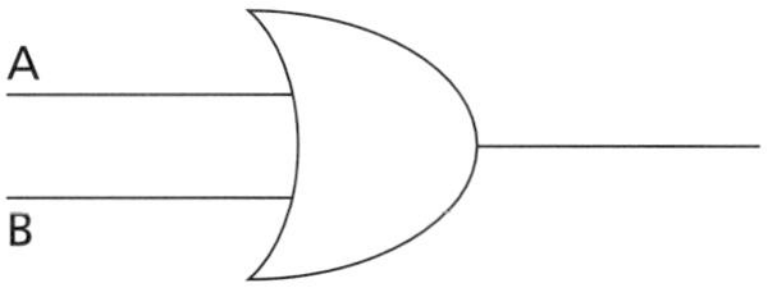

Input A	Input B	Output
0	0	0
0	1	1
1	0	1
1	1	1

A high input and another high or low input give a high output.

NAND gate

The NAND gate gives a **logic 1 output when input A or input B or both are not high.**

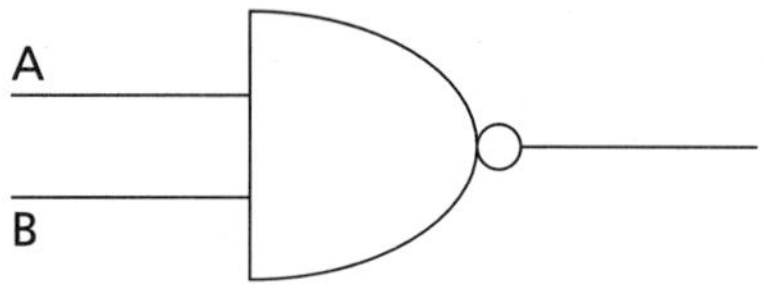

Input A	Input B	Output
0	0	1
0	1	1
1	0	1
1	1	0

A low input and another high or low input give a high output.

NOR gate

The NOR gate gives a **logic 1 output only when neither input A nor input B is high.**

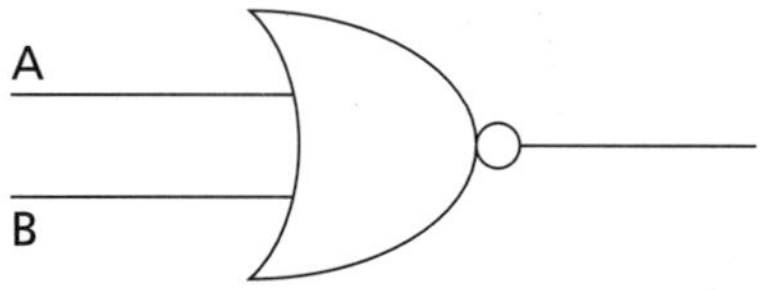

Input A	Input B	Output
0	0	1
0	1	0
1	0	0
1	1	0

Two low inputs give a high output.

(There is only a low current through logic gates, so you need an amplifier, such as a transistor, to drive a transducer. Alternatively you can use a reed relay to switch on a separate circuit.)

(Note: When drawing an alternating power supply (remember mains is a.c.) in a circuit, you do not draw a cell, but you draw a mini sine wave:

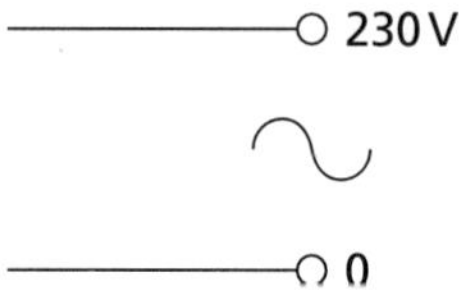

and label the appropriate voltage.)

Worked Questions

1. *Logic gates are set up as shown:*

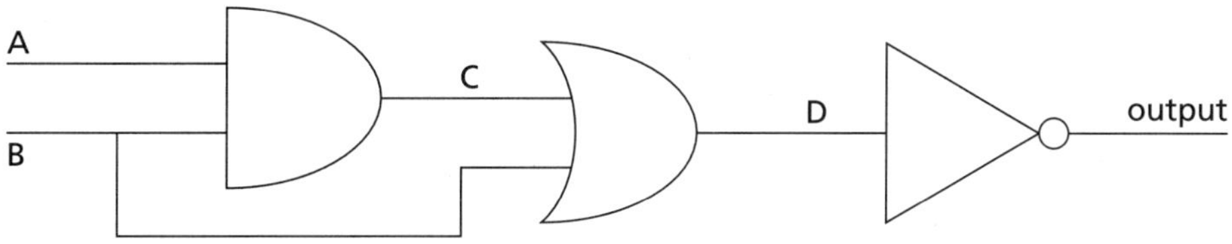

Complete the table below showing the outputs at various points of the circuit for different inputs. [12]

A	B	C	D	Output
0	0	0	0	1
0	1	0	1	0
1	0	0	0	1
1	1	1	1	0

This is just a case of thinking all the various stages through. Work out each column separately. A and B are easy; just the normal combinations. C is derived from these. D can then be worked out from B and C. Finally the output is whatever D isn't.

2. *An LED will give maximum brightness if a potential difference of 2 V is placed across it. In this situation, 200 mA flows. If a 9 V battery is to be used, find the appropriate value of R in the circuit shown here.* [3]

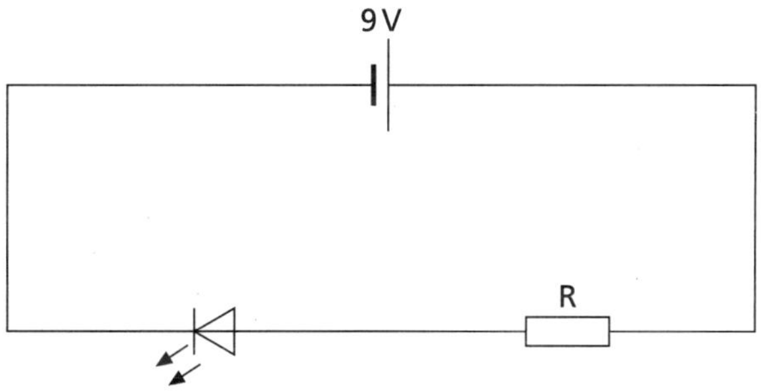

If the p.d. across the LED is 2 V, then the p.d. across the resistor has to be:

(9 – 2) = 7 V*
200 mA = 200/1000 A; 0.2 A flows in the circuit.

$V = IR \Rightarrow \frac{V}{I} = R$*

So, $R = \frac{7}{0.2}$

$= 35\ \Omega$

The appropriate value for the resistor would be 35 Ω.*

topic eight

nuclear physics

How to make an atomic bomb
Take two bits of uranium and bang them together. Believe that and not even this book can help you.

Atomic structure

Rutherford's (and Geiger's and Marsden's and William Kay's) gold-foil experiment

Rutherford fired alpha particles, which have a positive charge, at some very thin gold foil. Detectors had been placed around the foil, at different angles. Most particles went straight through, some were deflected, but a very few of them came straight back. Rutherford said it was 'like firing a fifteen-inch shell at a piece of tissue paper and having it come back and hit you'.

He concluded that atoms are mostly just empty space, which is why most of the alpha particles went straight through, but that at the centre, there was a very small **positively charged nucleus**, which deflected some of the particles. This nucleus contains 99.9% of the atom's mass.

Atom smallest distinguishable part of any element

Nuclei contain **protons** and **neutrons**, and **electrons** orbit the nucleus.
Protons and neutrons have almost the same mass; both have approximately 1840 times the mass of an electron.

Sodium, for example, has 11 protons. 11 is its **atomic number**. It usually has 12 neutrons. Therefore there are 23 particles in the nucleus, called **nucleons**. Its **mass number** is 23. The symbol for this sodium isotope (see below for explanation of *isotope*) is:

$^{A}_{Z}\,{}^{23}_{11}Na$

The mass number, A, is at the top; the atomic number, Z, is at the bottom.

Charge and ions

Protons have a charge of +1 unit; neutrons have no charge, and electrons have a charge of –1 unit. (The value of this unit of charge is 1.6×10^{-19} C.)

In an atom, the number of protons is equal to the number of electrons. However, atoms may lose one or more of their electrons or they may gain electrons. Losing or gaining electrons forms **ions**. The ion has a positive charge if there are more protons than electrons, and a negative charge if there are more electrons than protons.

Isotopes

Different isotopes of the same element have the same number of protons as each other, but different numbers of neutrons. For example:

$^{17}_{8}O$ is an oxygen isotope; $^{14}_{6}C$ is a carbon isotope.

The most common oxygen and carbon isotopes are $^{16}_{8}O$ and $^{12}_{6}C$ respectively.

Radioactive decay

Some types of nuclei are **unstable**, because the electrostatic forces pushing the protons apart are greater than the strong attractive nuclear forces between nucleons. Large nuclei are often unstable, with too many or too few neutrons.

Radioactive decay	spontaneous disintegration of unstable nuclei with emission of alpha (α), beta (β) or gamma (γ) radiation
Radioisotopes	radioactive isotopes

Ionising radiation

When radiation collides with neutral molecules or atoms, it makes them become charged by adding or removing electrons; in other words it **ionises** them. This is very harmful to living cells.

Radioactive decay equations

X and Y represent symbols for elements. A is the mass number, Z is the atomic number.

Alpha decay

The nucleus decays by emitting an **alpha particle**, which, like the nucleus of the helium atom, is composed of two neutrons and two protons.

$^{A}_{Z}X \rightarrow {}^{A-4}_{Z-2}Y + {}^{4}_{2}He$ or $^{A}_{Z}X \rightarrow {}^{A-4}_{Z-2}Y + {}^{4}_{2}\alpha$

Beta decay

A neutron in the nucleus turns into a proton and an electron. The electron is emitted as a **beta particle**.

$^{A}_{Z}X \rightarrow {}_{Z+1}{}^{A}Y + {}^{0}_{-1}\beta$

Gamma emission

Occurs when the nucleus emits an alpha or beta particle; the nucleus is in an excited state, so it loses surplus energy by emitting gamma radiation.

$(^{A}_{Z}X)^{EXCITED} \rightarrow {}^{A}_{Z}X$

The half-life

This is the time for half the atoms of a radioactive isotope to decay. For example, the radioactive carbon isotope, $^{14}_{6}C$ (carbon-14) has a half-life of 5730 years.

Take 10 000 atoms (hypothetically) of carbon-14.
After one half-life of 5730 years, there are about 5000 atoms of carbon-14 left.
After two half-lives, there are about 2500 atoms of carbon-14 left. This is a quarter of the original 10 000.
After three half-lives there are about 1250 atoms of carbon-14 left, an eighth of the original 10 000.

Detection of radioactivity

Alpha, beta and gamma radiation can be detected, with differing efficiencies, using the following methods, which all basically depend upon ionisation.

- **Photographic film** is blackened by alpha, beta and gamma radiation.
- In the **cloud chamber**, a ray from a radioactive source causes a line of ions on which a cloud trail forms. Only alpha radiation forms straight lines.
- The **Geiger–Müller tube (G–M tube)** is a metal tube, with a thin wire down the centre, and a very thin mica window at the front. It contains gas at low pressure. The principle is that gas at low pressure conducts electricity when ionised. Ionisation causes pulses of voltage which are detected by a device called a **scaler**. The scaler counts pulses, or the rate of pulses. The ratemeter shows counts per second. The G–M tube will detect background radiation as well as radiation from a source. Alpha, beta and gamma radiation are detected with differing efficiencies. (This also applies to photographic film and the cloud chamber.)

  Alpha radiation may also be detected using the:

- Gold-leaf electroscope. The leaf falls (or could rise) because of ionisation.

Activity a measure of the rate at which atoms decay; 1 becquerel (Bq) is a rate of decay of 1 nucleus per second

Alpha (α) radiation

- It consists of particles that are the same as helium nuclei, i.e. they are composed of two protons and two neutrons, and therefore positively charged.
- It is strongly ionising and very dangerous within the body.
- Alpha particles are stopped by paper or the thin layer of dead skin cells on the outside of the skin. They are also stopped by a few centimetres of air.
- Alpha particles are deflected slightly by electric and magnetic fields.
- The particles travel at one-tenth of the speed of light, typically.

Beta (β) radiation

- It consists of electrons emitted by the nucleus, and is therefore negatively charged (see diagram on p. 83).

- It is weakly ionising but still dangerous.
- Beta particles are stopped by aluminium a few millimetres in thickness.
- They are strongly deflected by electric and magnetic fields.
- They travel at speeds of up to half the speed of light.

Showing that beta radiation is negatively charged

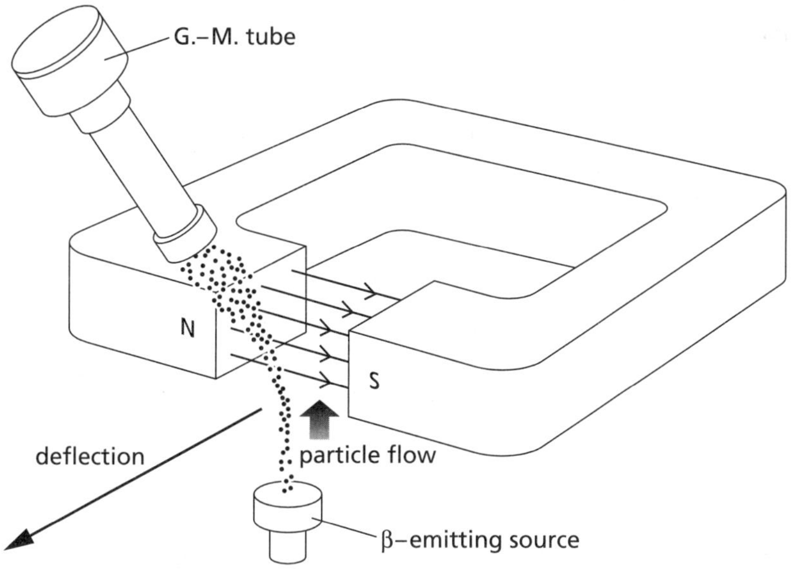

A source of beta radiation (conveniently but inaccurately shown here as visible particles!) is placed near to the magnetic field, as shown. The G–M tube is moved around above the field until it detects the radiation, and it is found that the charged particles have been deflected in the direction shown, because of the motor effect. Using the Left-hand Rule, the direction of the current must be downwards. However, this is conventional current direction from positive to negative, so the particles, which are travelling upwards from the source, are going from negative to positive. So the radiation must be negatively charged.

Gamma (γ) radiation

- The radiation is electromagnetic radiation of short wavelength.
- If the distance from the source doubles, then the intensity of the radiation decreases to a quarter. If the distance goes up by a factor of three, then the radiation intensity goes down by a factor of three squared, i.e. nine. This is an example of an **inverse-square law**.
- It is reduced (not stopped) by a block of lead (which is why sources are kept in lead cases).
- It is not affected by electric or magnetic fields.
- It travels at the speed of light in air.

Many people think alpha radiation is less dangerous than gamma radiation, because alpha radiation is less penetrating. This is not in fact true; although it is easily stopped, once inside the body, alpha radiation is so strongly ionising that it can cause serious damage. Gamma radiation tends to just go straight through you. However, it is still dangerous. No nuclear radiation is 'safe'.

Uses of radioisotopes

Detection

Radioactive tracers are used in medicine. They are used to perform scans; for example a patient breathes in a tiny amount of a radioactive gas, and then an X-ray is taken. Ionisation is damaging, so gamma rays (which do not ionise much) are used.

Testing and measurement

- Testing for wear in pipes and pistons, by monitoring the passage of a radioactive tracer.
- Thickness control. Beta particles are fired at the material to be measured. At a certain thickness, the correct level of radiation passes through.

Radioactive dating

If you know the half-life of a substance, and how much of it has decayed, then you can work out how old it is. For example, if the half-life is 2 years, and there is a quarter of the original amount of substance in a sample, then the sample is two half-lives old, i.e. 4 years. Carbon-14 (see Half-life section) is often used in this way to date ancient materials.

Irradiation of food

The radiation kills any bacteria.

Nuclear energy

Unstable uranium-235 nuclei are bombarded with slow-moving neutrons. Each atom which is hit by a neutron splits into two roughly equal parts and emits two or three fast-moving neutrons; this is called **nuclear fission**. Energy is released, mostly as the kinetic energy of the fission fragments. The neutrons released hit more uranium-235 nuclei, producing even more neutrons, and so on; this is a **chain reaction**.

Naturally occurring uranium has only a very small amount of uranium-235 and a large amount of the stable isotope uranium-238, so for a chain reaction to happen the uranium fuel has to be **enriched** with uranium-235. In a nuclear reactor the enriched fuel is about 3% uranium-235 and 97% uranium-238. There also has to be a **moderator**, usually made of graphite or water, to slow the neutrons down; this makes them more likely to be captured by a uranium-235 nucleus.

If the mass of uranium is greater than a certain **critical mass**, then the chain reaction may take place very quickly – an atom bomb.

The mass present before each fission of a nucleus is greater than the mass present after the fission. This lost mass is converted to energy. How much energy is given by Einstein's famous equation:

Energy released = mass lost × speed of light squared

$$E = mc^2$$

The amount of energy released by the decay of a single nucleus is very small; as Rutherford said 'The energy from a nucleus is a poor thing indeed'. However, in a reaction as such the fission in an atomic bomb, billions and billions of nuclei are decaying, so a lot of energy is released.

Nuclear power station

The **reactor core** contains fuel rods, moderators, and **control rods**, made of boron or cadmium, which absorb neutrons. The control rods can be lowered into the reactor to slow down the chain reaction or stop it. The reactor is shielded in steel and concrete, to absorb gamma rays.

The reactor core is at red heat. A coolant, such as carbon dioxide gas or pressurised water is pumped through the reactor core. The coolant takes away heat to the **heat exchanger** where water is boiled to produce steam. This, at high pressure, turns a turbine which drives a generator to produce electricity.

Worked Questions

A scientist, while playing at home in his garage extension, used a Geiger–Müller tube (an electronic counter) to study three different types of radioactive materials, labelled A, B, and C.

The scientist placed each sample 0.02 m from the Geiger–Müller tube and recorded the following results:

Material between source and G–M tube	Count rate (counts/minute)		
	A	B	C
0.5 cm of lead	20	22	106
0.2 cm of aluminium	23	103	149
Paper (one sheet)	30	182	171
No barrier	79	197	172

Having removed the samples, the scientist observed that the Geiger–Müller tube was still recording about 20 counts per minute.

1. *What was causing the final reading of 20 counts per minute?* [1]

   Naturally occurring background radiation.

You can almost always count on there being a question on background radiation just like the one above, and if not, it will be incorporated somehow into a longer question. The message is to think of background radiation hand-in-hand with a radiation question.

2. *What was the effect of the sheet of paper on the radiation from source A?* [1]

   Much of the radiation was blocked out.

3. *What difference did the lead make to the readings from source B?* [1]

   Again, the reading was reduced because much of the radiation was blocked out.

4. *Use the scientist's results to name the radiation emitted by the samples, giving reasons. (Assume that only one type of radiation is coming from each source.)* [6]

Source A is alpha radiation, because the radioactive particles are even stopped by the sheet of paper.
Source B is beta radiation. The radioactive particles are blocked by the aluminium sheet but they aren't blocked by the paper sheet.
Source C is gamma radiation. This radiation is not greatly affected by the barriers. It is capable of penetrating most substances.

A nuclear scientist is conducting an experiment in which alpha particles are fired at a sheet of gold which is only one atom thick. The diagram shows an event, at atomic level, during the experiment.

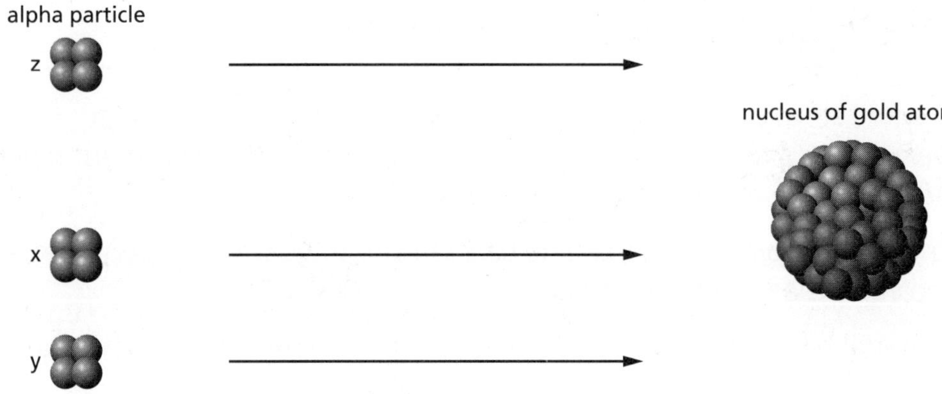

The isotope of gold used is $^{197}_{79}Au$.

5. *How many neutrons does the gold nucleus have?* [1]

197 – 79 = 118
A (mass number) – Z (atomic number) = number of neutrons.

6. *How many electrons does the gold atom have?* [1]

79
In an atom the number of electrons is the same as the number of protons.

7. *What is the relative charge of the gold nucleus?* [1]

+79
Positive. It contains only protons which are positive and neutrons which are neutral.

8. *Describe and explain the path of the alpha particle x as it approaches the gold nucleus?* [2]

The particle will be deflected straight back, but will not touch the gold nucleus. An alpha particle consists of two protons and two neutrons and thus is positively charged.* As the nucleus is also positively charged the two repel each other* and the lighter alpha particle is deflected straight back.

You have to make sure with questions like these that you don't simply describe what happens and forget to answer the explanation part of the question. You may not think this is a point worth making but it is a sad fact that many people lose marks by omission rather than error.

9. *If particle z is slightly deflected describe the path of y.* [1]

   y is deflected more than z but in the opposite direction to the deflection of z.

10. *98% of the alpha particles were detected on the opposite side of the foil from the source of the particles. What does this suggest about the structure of gold?* [2]

    As few particles have been deflected back, there must be large spaces between each nucleus for the alpha particles to pass through.

topic nine

thermal physics

The kinetic theory of matter

The kinetic theory of matter states that matter is composed of particles (ions, atoms, molecules) that are in random motion. Evidence for the kinetic theory comes from diffusion and Brownian motion.

Diffusion the net random movement of particles from an area where they are high in concentration to an area where they are low in concentration

For example, if a little liquid bromine is placed in a glass diffusion tube and left for a few minutes, the tube will become filled with orange-brown gaseous bromine. (Bromine is **volatile**; it has a boiling point close to room temperature.) The kinetic theory explains this by saying that the bromine gas is made up of molecules that are moving randomly. It is more likely that a bromine molecule will move from a place where there are many bromine molecules, to a place where there are fewer molecules, than the other way round. Therefore, more molecules move in the direction of the lower concentration of bromine. The net result is the spreading out of the bromine gas throughout the tube.

(Bromine liquid and bromine vapour are both very dangerous, and your teacher will use a special bromine diffusion apparatus and specific safety measures if he or she demonstrates this effect.)

If you haven't seen bromine in action, an air freshener works in the same way. Particles of air-freshening matter diffuse from one point to fill the whole room, not just staying in one area, giving you weeks of fresh air goodness.

Brownian motion is the effect observed if you look through a microscope at some illuminated smoke particles. The smoke particles will appear to be jumping around and moving in random directions. The kinetic theory explains this by saying that air molecules are colliding with the smoke particles and this is what causes the jumping around effect. Brownian motion was originally observed by Robert Brown in 1827. He was looking at pollen grains, suspended in water.

There are electrostatic forces between particles in a solid or liquid. If you squeeze a solid, you feel the repulsive forces; if you stretch it, you feel the attractive forces.

There are three states of matter: **solid**, **liquid** and **gas**.

Solids

The molecules are tightly packed. The distance between the centres of particles is approximately one diameter. The molecule vibrates about a fixed position. (This means it has kinetic energy and it is this energy that we call heat.) A solid has a fixed shape, a fixed volume and cannot be compressed.

Liquids

The molecules are also tightly packed, and again there is about one diameter distance between the centres, but the molecules can move about at random, and vibrate a little. If the liquid is heated and its temperature rises, the molecules move around more quickly, i.e. their kinetic energy increases. Liquids have a fixed volume, a variable shape (they will take up the shape of their container) and are very slightly compressible.

Gases

The molecules effectively have no interactions (in the form of electrostatic forces) between each other. The distance between them is typically 10 diameters, but this depends on the pressure in the room. The particles are completely free from each other, and are moving randomly. If the gas is heated, the molecules move more quickly. Gases have a variable volume, a variable shape, will fill and take up the shape of a container and are easily compressed.

Conduction, convection and radiation

These are different methods of transferring heat or thermal energy.

Conduction

Conduction the transfer of heat energy through a material without the material itself moving

Energy is passed on from particle to particle; the increasingly energetic vibrations of the particles are passed along. Conduction requires a **medium**, a material to carry vibrations. There is no conduction in a vacuum such as the vacuum in the wall of a Thermos® flask.

All metals are good conductors of heat, because of their structure: metal ions are held together by a 'sea' of electrons that are called **delocalised** (or **free**) **electrons**. These electrons are very free-moving, and not only are they charge carriers (so that metals are also good electrical conductors), but they allow another method of conducting heat as well as the vibration of particles. **Insulators** (that is, poor conductors of heat) do not have these delocalised electrons.

Most liquids are poor conductors of heat. (An exception? Mercury!)

Insulation
Air is an important insulator. Wool contains pockets of trapped air, and this stops heat being conducted away from the body.

A refrigerator has insulating material around it to stop heat energy being conducted in.

It is most useful to insulate the roof of a house as this is where most of the heat energy escapes. A measure of the degree of insulation a material can give is called the *U*-value. It's units are W/(m^2 degree C) or watts (joules per second) per square metre per degree Celsius.

Thermal energy lost per second = U-value × area of heat loss × temperature difference

For example, an uninsulated roof has a U-value of 2.0 W/(m^2 degree C). If the roof was 10 m × 10 m, the temperature inside was 20°C, and the temperature outside was 5°C, then:

Temperature difference = 20 – 5 = 15 degree C

Thermal energy lost per second = (2.0 W/(m^2 degree C)) × 100 m^2 × 15 degree C
= 3000 joules per second

For an insulated roof with a U-value of 0.4 W/(m^2 degree C), with the same area and at the same temperature difference:

Thermal energy lost per second = (0.4 W/(m^2 degree C)) × 100 m^2 × 15 degree C
= 600 joules per second

Convection

Convection the transfer of thermal energy through a liquid or gas by movement of the liquid or gas particles themselves

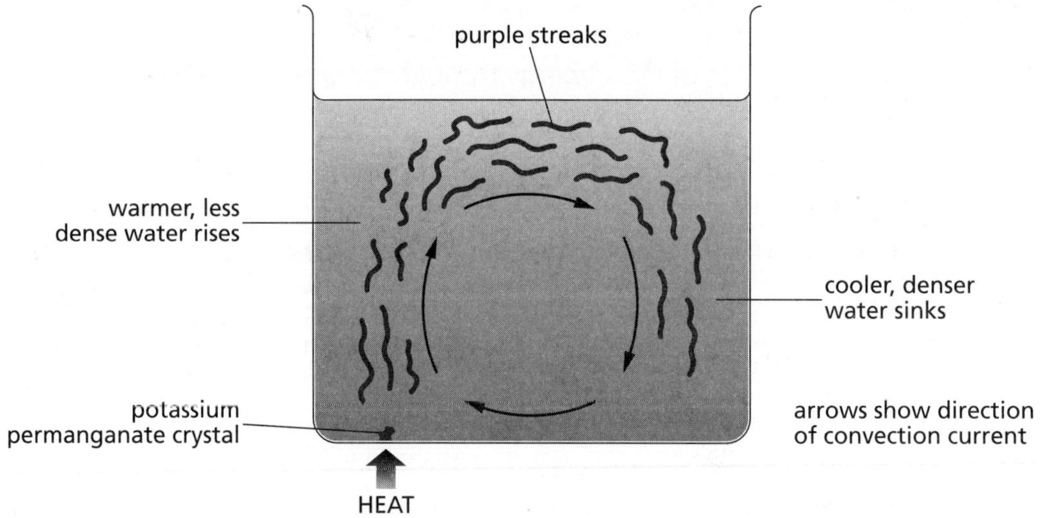

A potassium permanganate crystal (a purple crystal) is placed at the bottom of a beaker of water. Near the crystal, the water is purple, where part of the crystal dissolves. The beaker is heated with a small Bunsen flame, near the crystal only. The water around the crystal heats up. Its temperature increases, and its density decreases. This is because when particles have more energy, they move about more and take up more space. When they take up more space, there will be fewer particles for a given volume. As its density decreases, you can see the purple-coloured water rise. The cooler denser water sinks, the warmer water rises, and a **convection current** has been set up. The purple colour has moved around with the water, so you see a trail of purple.

'Radiators' actually heat by convection: the colder air sinks and the warmer air rises, so that thermal energy is transferred by movement of the air.

The Sun causes convection currents. During daytime, the Sun warms up the land more quickly than the sea. (The land also cools down more quickly at night.) The warmer air above the heated land rises and cooler air from the sea moves over the land. At night, the sea is warmer than the land so the cooler air over the land moves out to sea. Glider pilots use these convection currents.

Radiation

This is the transfer of heat by electromagnetic waves. (All bodies give out heat, i.e. they emit radiation.)

Dull black surfaces are good radiators, and also good absorbers of radiation (which is why wearing dark clothes makes you feel hotter on a sunny day).

Shiny light-coloured surfaces are bad radiators and bad absorbers of radiation, as they reflect the waves.

The greenhouse effect and global warming

- Short-wavelength infrared radiation from the Sun enters through the Earth's atmosphere. The Earth absorbs some of this radiation. The radiation that is re-emitted by the Earth is long-wavelength infrared.
- Long-wavelength infrared waves are not able to pass through the so-called 'greenhouse gases', such as carbon dioxide and methane, in the atmosphere. Instead, they get reflected back towards the Earth.
- This trapping of long-wave infrared radiation by the Earth's atmosphere is called the greenhouse effect, because it resembles what happens in greenhouses; infrared goes in but does not come out. This leads to the overall warming of the greenhouse, or the Earth – contributing to global warming.
- An additional greenhouse effect, caused by the carbon dioxide from the burning of fossil fuels, may be leading to an average temperature rise across the entire Earth. Even if this were a rise of only a few degrees, it would be enough to melt the polar ice caps, and cause flooding in low-lying areas of the Earth.

The Thermos® flask

The flask is double-walled. The vacuum between the walls stops thermal energy loss via conduction and convection, as there is no medium. Radiation can travel in a vacuum, so both the walls are made of glass, with silvering, so that radiation is reflected. The first wall reduces radiation; the second reflects any rays that may have passed through. Most of the heat loss is through the cap, as this is the part which is least well insulated.

Boiling point and melting point

Impurities in a substance raise its boiling point, and lower its melting point.

Putting salt on icy roads lowers the melting point of the ice, and it thaws.

Pressure on a substance lowers the melting point.

If a thin wire is placed on a block of ice, with each end of the wire tied to a heavy mass, then the pressure caused by the wire on the ice causes the ice to melt. The wire slowly moves down through the ice. The ice above the wire refreezes, as there is no pressure on it. When the wire has completely cut through the ice, the ice is still intact, as the ice above the wire has frozen.

As pressure decreases, the boiling point is lowered.

Thus, cups of tea made on high mountains may be boiling, but not very hot. Blood would boil in a vacuum (as pressure is effectively zero) which is why space suits are pressurised.

A **pressure cooker** increases pressure, so that when the water is boiling, it is at a higher temperature than usual. At normal pressure, no matter how long you heat the water, it would not exceed 100°C, as this is when it boils, and the temperature stops rising. In a pressure cooker, the water boils at about 120°C, so food cooks quicker.

Latent heat

Evaporation causes cooling. Faster molecules near the surface of the liquid are able to escape from the attractive forces of the other molecules and leave the liquid. As the more energetic molecules escape, the average kinetic energy of the remaining molecules goes down, i.e. the liquid cools. The extra energy needed by the molecules to escape from the liquid is called **latent heat of vaporisation**. Similarly, when a substance changes from solid to liquid, the molecules need to take in energy from the surroundings. This is called **latent heat of melting**.

Worked Questions

1. *Complete the table below describing solids, liquids and gases* [4]

	Forces between particles	*Energy and structure*
Solids	Strong forces of attraction between particles.	Kinetic and potential energy of particles causes them to vibrate about a fixed position in the lattice.
Liquids	Strong forces of attraction between particles.*	Particles have enough energy to move through the structure while vibrating,* but do not break free completely.*
Gases	No forces of attraction between particles.*	Particles have enough kinetic energy to break free.

This question is purely a memory one. It is still useful, however, to make note of the wording used to describe the forces of attraction and the atomic structure. Many students find it difficult to put their knowledge into words.

The diagram below shows a bath with three rods pushed through the side of it. The bath contains boiling water. Each rod has a ball-bearing stuck to it with wax, at the opposite end from the bath. Eventually, the wax will melt and the ball-bearings will fall.

Plan view

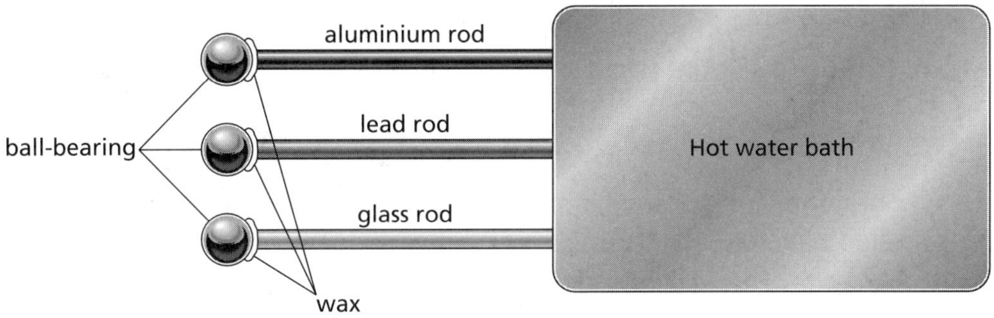

2. *Which ball falls first?* [1]

   The ball on the aluminium rod. This is because aluminium conducts heat better than the other two materials.*

3. *Name and describe the process by which thermal energy is transferred along the lead rod.* [3]

   Conduction.* The free electrons in the metal have an increase in kinetic energy and move rapidly to cooler parts of the rod where they transfer their kinetic energy by colliding with atoms.* Also, as heat energy reaches an atom, it begins to vibrate more energetically. It passes on some of its increased energy to the neighbouring atom which also begins to vibrate more energetically and so on, and heat energy is passed along the rod.*

Remember that the main way heat is conducted in metals is by the free electrons. It is likely that you will lose a mark if you refer to them only as 'particles'.

4. *Why are metals good conductors (in both electrical and thermal senses)?* [3]

   Metal atoms donate their outer shell of electrons to a 'sea' of delocalised electrons,* which are free-moving. These fast-moving delocalised electrons rapidly transfer thermal energy,* and so metals are good conductors of heat. The electrons also carry charge,* and so metals are good conductors of electricity.

These questions show you the style of the exam question and the type of answer the examiner hopes to see on the page. Economise with your words. Do not miss anything out, but be concise as well.

topic nine-and-a-half

the Earth and beyond

Life, the universe and everything

(Some of the information in this section is obvious; however, it's here because it's in the syllabus.)

The Universe

Our Sun is one of millions of stars in the Universe. The stars are clustered together in groups called **galaxies**. There are at least a billion galaxies in the Universe and quite possibly more. The galaxies in the Universe are millions of times further apart than the stars they contain, and the stars in the galaxies are normally millions of times further apart than the planets are from the stars.

Stars

Stars like the Sun are constantly changing at a very slow rate. The very high temperatures cause stars to expand and the huge mass of each star causes it to contract, by gravitational attraction. In the main period of a star's life these two forces cancel each other out and the star will remain in a stable state for billions of years. After a certain amount of time, which is different for each star, the forces causing it to expand start to win and the star grows in size to become a **red giant**. At this point two things can happen. The star may grow to a size where gravity causes the core to compact into a **white dwarf** becoming millions of times denser than anything on Earth. If the red giant is particularly massive then it may rapidly contract, resulting in an explosion, to become a **supernova**. The explosion throws enormous amounts of gas, dust and radiation into space. Often a very dense **neutron star** remains. A neutron star is essentially a strange fluid composed entirely of neutrons. Much of a normal atom is just empty space; its mass is concentrated in the minute (compared to the rest of the atom) nucleus. However, the fluid of which a neutron star is made does not have these large gaps, so the star is very dense.

The energy radiated by stars is generated through **nuclear fusion** (completely different from nuclear fission). The process of nuclear fusion consists of two nuclei of lighter elements combining to form nuclei of heavy elements. In the case of most stars, hydrogen nuclei fuse together to form helium nuclei.

The nuclei of some of the heaviest atoms are thought to be only produced in the centre of stars. These heavy nuclei are found on planets in the solar system, suggesting that the planets are formed from gas and dust which includes the remnants of exploded stars.

The 'big bang'

It is widely agreed that the Universe probably began with a huge explosion: the 'big bang'. The evidence for this theory is as follows.

The light that reaches Earth from other galaxies tends towards the red end of the spectrum (see topic two – waves). This is called **red shift**. What is actually happening in terms of light waves, is that as the source travels further away, the wavelength lengthens. This is best (and most often) demonstrated with sound waves. Imagine a police car coming towards you at high speed, with the siren blaring. As it approaches, the pitch of the wailing siren gets higher. The sound waves are effectively 'compressed' so that the wavelength is shorter. A shorter wavelength in a sound wave makes the pitch high. As the police car speeds away from you, the pitch of the siren will decrease. The wavelength of the sound waves has increased. This is called the **Doppler effect**.

The radiation emitted from galaxies behaves in a similar manner. If a galaxy is moving towards us (this is purely hypothetical, by the way, you shouldn't worry about a head-on collision with Andromeda) then the wavelength of the light from the galaxy would be shorter, just as the pitch of the siren gets higher as the car comes towards you. So the spectrum of light would be shifted towards the blue end, as blue light has the shortest wavelength. This is called **blue shift**.

If the galaxy is moving away from us, then the wavelength of the light has a longer wavelength (like the pitch of the siren getting lower as the car moves away). Red light has the longest wavelength, so the spectrum of light from the galaxy is shifted towards the red end.

A most amazing discovery, made by Edwin Hubble, was that all distant galaxies displayed red shift. He also showed that the amount of red shift was greater, the more distant the galaxy. In other words, the galaxies that were furthest away were also moving away the fastest.

So, the best way of explaining the red shift from galaxies is that the universe is expanding. This may have started millions of years ago, from a single, infinitesimally small point, with a huge explosion that brought the universe as we know it into being. Hence the name 'big bang'.

Our Solar System

Originally it was thought that the Earth was the centre of the Universe and that all the other heavenly bodies (stars, the Moon, other planets and the Sun), orbited around the Earth. This was disproved by observations of the movement of these heavenly bodies that showed the Earth and other planets to orbit the Sun.

The other planets, like Earth, do not give off light; they are visible because they reflect light from the Sun.

From our position on Earth, the other stars in our galaxy seem to stay in fixed patterns which are called **constellations**. However, the planets in the Solar System, which look exactly like stars from this distance, can be distinguished from the stars by their slow movement across the fixed constellations. This is because the stars are at immense distances from us – Proxima Centauri, the nearest star after the Sun, is over 4 light-years away – while the planets are 'near' in comparison. Where we see the planets against the constellations depends on where the planets are in relation to the Earth in their orbits round the Sun.

The planets of the Solar System all move around the Sun in the same direction. Their orbits are all roughly in the same plane as the Earth's and almost circular (except Pluto's). It takes the Earth 1 year ($365\frac{1}{4}$ days) to orbit the Sun. The further a planet is from the Sun, the longer it takes to complete one orbit.

It takes the Earth 24 hours to spin once about its own axis. Other planets may take much longer or much less time to complete one spin on their own axis.

How do bodies stay in orbit?

Any two bodies attract each other with the force of gravity; this is what causes us to stay on the Earth and the planets to orbit the Sun. The greater the mass of a body the greater force of gravity it exerts; the further apart two objects are the smaller the force of gravity will be between them. It is like magnets: when two unlike poles are put close to each other, they are pulled together more strongly than when they are far apart. (This is a good way of visualising 'gravity' but is technically wrong; do not quote it in an exam.)

Satellites and planets stay in orbit around larger bodies due to a combination of the speed of the smaller body and the force of gravity between the two bodies. To stay in orbit at a particular distance the smaller body must be moving at a particular speed. The further away an orbiting body, is the longer it takes to orbit.

The orbits of the planets around the sun are ellipses (squashed circles) with the Sun quite close to the centre.

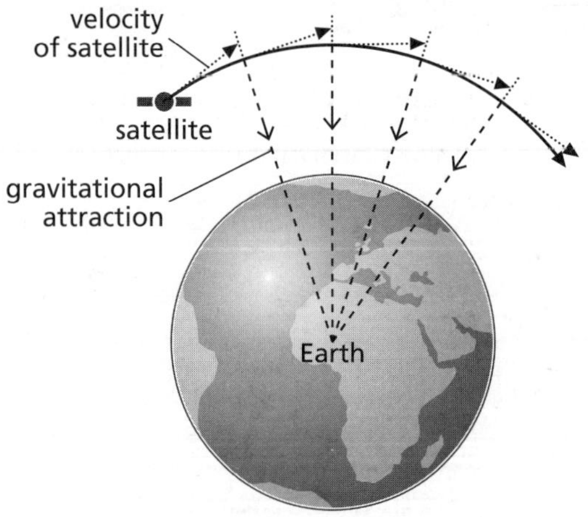

Comets have orbits which are far from circular; because they are small in comparison with other bodies in space, they are affected by the gravity of many sources to a greater extent. Sometimes their orbits take them near to the Sun and Earth and this is when they can be seen.

Artificial satellites

These are put into orbit for various tasks, of which you need to know a few examples:

- To send data between places on Earth which are too far away from each other to send messages by other means.
- To view the Universe without the distortions caused by the Earth's atmosphere.
- To monitor the weather on Earth.
- To conduct geological surveys.
- For satellite TV.
- As spy satellites, to take aerial photos.
- To rain laser death from above. Sorry to disappoint, but this last one is a lie.

Satellites which are used for monitoring are put into **low polar orbits**, passing over both Poles within a few hours. This means that they pass over a large portion of the Earth each day. Satellites intended for communication purposes are set in a **geostationary orbit**, which means an orbit high above the Equator, so that they move around the Earth at the same rate at which it spins. This means that when viewed from the Earth they always appear in the same position.

Worked Questions

1. *By considering the motion of the Earth, explain the meaning of:* [2]
   a) A year
   b) A day

   A year is the time it takes for the Earth to move around the Sun exactly once.
   One day is the time it takes for the Earth to spin on its axis exactly once.

2. *What is the force of attraction between the Moon and the Earth?* [1]

   Gravity

3. *Name two factors that this force depends on.* [2]

   Masses of bodies.
   Distance between bodies.

4. *How many planets are there in the Solar System?* [0]

   9

That question was too easy to be worth any marks.

> *(Stop press: There is at the moment (January 1999) a big debate about whether Pluto should be classified as a planet. So instead of being 'too easy', this is now a trick question; a turnaround which often happens as physics develops. However, you won't get any trick questions in your exam. Good luck!)*

appendix a

Laws and equations

topic one – mechanics

$v = \frac{s}{t}$

$a = \frac{\Delta v}{\Delta t} = \frac{v - u}{t}$ — Δ means 'change in'

$v = u + at$

$s = ut + \frac{1}{2}at^2$

$v^2 - u^2 = 2as$

$s = \left(\frac{u + v}{2}\right)t$

s	displacement	metre (m)
u	initial velocity	metre per second (m/s)
v	final velocity	metre per second (m/s)
a	acceleration	metre per second squared (m/s²)
t	time	second (s)

$W = Fs$

W	work	joule (J)
F	force	newton (N)
s	distance	metre (m)

Energy can never be created or destroyed; only converted from one form to another.

$W = mg$

W	weight	newton (N)
g	gravitational field strength	newton per kilogram (N/kg)
m	mass	kilogram (kg)

$\Sigma F = ma$ (for a constant mass)

F	force	newton (N)
m	mass	kilogram (kg)
a	acceleration	metre per second squared (m/s²)
Σ	means total (in this case resultant external force)	

$Moment = Fs$

F	force	newton (N)
s	perpendicular distance from pivot	metre (m)

Total anticlockwise moment = total clockwise moment

$p = mv$

p	momentum	kilogram metre per second (kg m/s)
m	mass	kilogram (kg)
v	velocity	metre per second (m/s)

The force on a body is equal to the rate of change of its momentum
so that:

$F = \frac{mv - mu}{t}$	mv	final momentum	kilogram metre per second (kg m/s)
	mu	initial momentum	kilogram metre per second (kg m/s)
	t	time	second (s)
$Ft = mv - mu$	Ft	impulse	kilogram metre

Total momentum before collision = total momentum after collision
provided no external forces are acting.

$KE = \frac{1}{2}mv^2$	KE	kinetic energy	joule (J)
$GPE = mg\Delta h$	m	mass	kilogram (kg)
	v	velocity	metre per second (m/s)
	GPE	gravitational potential energy	joule (J)
	g	gravitational field strength	newton per kilogram (N/kg)
	Δh	change in height	metre (m)

$P = \frac{W}{t}$	P	power	watt (W)
	W	work done (energy change)	joule (J)
	t	time	second (s)

$$\text{Efficiency} = \frac{\text{useful energy output}}{\text{total energy input}} = \frac{\text{power output}}{\text{power input}}$$

Multiply your answer by 100 to give a percentage

$\rho = \frac{\text{mass}}{\text{volume}}$ ρ density kilogram per cubic metre (kg/m^3)

Hooke's law: extension of a spring $\propto$ force applied, up to the elastic limit.
$\propto$ means 'is proportional to'.

$P = \frac{F}{A}$	F	force	newton (N)
	A	area	square metre (m^2)
	P	pressure	newton per metre squared (N/m^2) or pascal (Pa)

$P = h\rho g$	h	depth	metre (m)
	ρ	density of the fluid	kilogram per metre cubed (kg/m^3)
	g	gravitational field strength	newton per kilogram (N/kg)

Newton's Laws of Motion:

1. *If a mass has no resultant forces or moments acting upon it, then it stays at rest or keeps moving in a straight line at constant speed.*
2. *The resultant force is proportional to the rate of change of momentum. This is more usually quoted at GCSE as $\sum F = ma$.*
3. *Every action has an equal and opposite reaction.*

topic two – waves

$f = \frac{1}{T}$	T	time period	second (s)
	f	frequency	hertz (Hz)
$v = f\lambda$	v	velocity of wave	metre per second (m/s)
	f	frequency	hertz (Hz)
	λ	wavelength	metre (m)

topic three – optics

Angle of incidence = angle of reflection

$\angle i = \angle r$

$$\text{Refractive index of substance} = \frac{\text{speed of light in air}}{\text{speed of light in substance}}$$

$$\text{Refractive index} = \frac{\text{real depth}}{\text{apparent depth}}$$

$\frac{1}{f} = \frac{1}{v} + \frac{1}{u}$	f	focal length	metre (m)
	v	image distance	metre (m)
	u	object distance	metre (m)

Note that for virtual images, v is negative

$$\text{Power of a lens} = \frac{1}{f}$$

The unit is dioptres when f is in metres.

topic four – electricity

Like charges repel, opposite charges attract

$Q = It$

$V = \frac{W}{Q}$	W	energy converted	joule (J)
	V	potential difference	volt (V)
	Q	charge	coulomb (C)

Kirchhoff's First Law: The total current flowing into a junction is the same as the sum of the currents flowing out of it.

$$\text{Resistance} = \frac{\text{potential difference}}{\text{current}}$$

$R = \dfrac{V}{I}$	R	resistance	ohm (Ω)
	V	potential difference	volt (V)
	I	current	ampere (A)

$V = IR$

Resistance $\propto$ length

$$\text{Resistance} \propto \frac{1}{\text{cross-sectional area}}$$

Where something is proportional to 1/something else, it is called **inversely proportional**.

In series, the total resistance, R_T

$R_T = R_1 + R_2 + R_3 + \ldots$

In parallel, to find the total resistance, use:

$$\frac{1}{R_T} = \frac{1}{R_1} + \frac{1}{R_2} + \frac{1}{R_3} + \ldots$$

$P = VI$	P	power	watt (W)
	V	potential difference	volt (V)
	I	current	ampere (A)

topic five – electricity and magnetism

Like poles repel, unlike poles attract

The Right-hand Grip Rule: If a wire carrying a current is gripped in the right hand, with the thumb pointing in the direction of the conventional current, then the fingers indicate the sense (direction) of the magnetic field.

Fleming's Left-hand Rule, for the Motor Effect: If the thumb, the first finger, and the second finger of the left hand are held at right angles to each other, then:

*the **F**irst finger points in the direction of the **F**ield (N – S)*
*the se**C**ond finger points in the direction of conventional **C**urrent (+ve to –ve)*
*the thu**M**b points in the direction of the **M**otion of the conductor.*

This is because (or basically a better way to remember that) charges moving at right angles to a magnetic field experience a force at right angles to their motion (the direction of the current) and to the magnetic field.

topic six – electromagnetic induction

Fleming's Right-hand Rule, for the Dynamo Effect: If the thumb, the first finger, and the second finger of the right hand are held at right angles to each other, then:

*the **F**irst finger points in the direction of the **F**ield (N – S)*
*the se**C**ond finger points in the direction of conventional **C**urrent (+ve to –ve)*
*the thu**M**b points in the direction of the **M**otion of the conductor.*

Faraday's Law: The size of the induced voltage is proportional to the rate at which magnetic field lines are cut.

Lenz's Law: The direction of a current induced by the dynamo effect is such as to oppose the change that caused the induced current.

Transformer equation:

$$\frac{V_s}{V_p} = \frac{n_s}{n_p} = \frac{I_p}{I_s}$$

n_p number of turns in primary coil
n_s number of turns in secondary coil
V_p p.d. across primary coil
V_s p.d. across secondary coil
I_p current in primary coil
I_s current in secondary coil

assuming 100% efficiency.

Power to primary = Power to secondary, assuming 100% efficiency

If $n_p < n_s$ the transformer is **step-up**; the voltage in the secondary coil is greater than in the primary if there are more turns on the secondary coil.

If $n_p > n_s$ the transformer is **step-down**; the voltage in the secondary coil is less than in the primary if there are fewer turns on the secondary coil.

topic seven – electronics

The potential divider equation (with reference to the diagram on page 72)

$$V_1 = \left(\frac{R_1}{R_1 + R_2}\right) \times V$$

topic eight – nuclear physics

Alpha decay

$${}^{A}_{Z}\mathrm{X} \rightarrow {}^{A-4}_{Z-2}\mathrm{Y} + {}^{4}_{2}\mathrm{He} \text{ (or } {}^{4}_{2}\alpha)$$

Beta decay

$${}^{A}_{Z}\mathrm{X} \rightarrow {}_{Z+1}{}^{A}\mathrm{Y} + {}^{0}_{-1}\beta$$

A neutron in the nucleus turns into a proton and an electron. The electron is emitted as a beta particle.

Gamma emission

$({}^{A}_{Z}X)^{EXCITED} \rightarrow {}^{A}_{Z}X$

$E = mc^2$	E	energy released	joule (J)
	m	mass	kilogram (kg)
	c	speed of light	metre per second (m/s)

Activity is measured in becquerels
1 becquerel (Bq) = 1 nucleus decaying per second

topic nine – thermal physics

Heat lost per second = *U*-value × area of heat loss × temperature difference

heat lost per second	watts (W)
U-value	watts per square metre per degree Celsius (W/m^2 degree C)
area of heat loss	square metre (m^2)
temperature difference	degree (degree C)

appendix b

Hints and tips

1. Read and then re-read the question. Look for the meaning of the question carefully by finding **key words**. (Remember that there is a difference between 'describe' and 'explain'.) Make sure you have fully answered the question.

2. **Write legibly**: the examiner's not going to give you the benefit of the doubt for something s/he can't read.

3. As soon as you read a question, try to think of the key points that go with the topic. For example, if a question is asked about electromagnetic induction that says something like 'Why does the bulb flash' your thought processes should have immediately brought to you the words 'changing magnetic field' which is associated with everything in electromagnetic induction.

4. The examiners are marking according to very strict mark schemes, and they follow them to the letter. The mark scheme is looking for very specific key words or phrases. For example, a question that asks you how a transformer works, for 3 marks, is looking for three points:

   a) primary current produces a magnetic field in iron core
   b) magnetic field passes through secondary coil
   c) magnetic field changes and induces current in secondary coil.

   Being aware of this allows you to make extremely **concise** answers. Examiners hate waffle. Usually there is a mark per point for a simple question; for a long question it's a mark per point plus a mark for each explanation, and for calculations it's a mark per significant step plus a mark for the correct method/equation, and its correct use, and finally a mark for the right answer, quoted to a reasonable degree of accuracy.

5. Calculations: you must **write down the equation or law you are using**. You will get a mark for writing the correct equation, as the examiner knows you know what you're doing. Even if you get everything else wrong (which you should try not to do) then you will at least get some of the marks. Never take for granted that the examiners will assume you know simple facts: *show them!*

6. Quote your answers to a sensible degree of accuracy. Think how stupid an answer like 'Height of ball = 2.71828182846 m' is. Three significant figures is usually a good value to stick with; otherwise give your answer to the accuracy the data is given to.

7. Think about how sensible your answers are. If you get an answer like 'speed of projectile = 400 000 000 m/s' then think again. (How could it be faster than the speed of light? And don't you start about the Einstein–Podolsky–Rosen paradox.)

8. **Don't forget your units.**

9. Stick to SI units as much as possible; no, for *everything*. If the question does not give you SI units, **convert the data into SI units** before you do any calculations.

10. If you get stuck on a question, then abandon it. You'll find that in most cases, if you start doing the other questions that you can do, it will increase your confidence, and you may just be able to have a good stab at the hard one after you have gone and got the easy marks. Also, it gives your subconscious mind time to do the question. Your subconscious is usually better at exams than your conscious mind. Why do you think that you solve Dingbats when you stop thinking about them? If you are really stuck, picture your teacher in your mind, and ask him/her for the solution.

11. Always check the sign of an answer. If you don't it could end up sending you in the wrong direction. If you take a system, say throwing a ball in the air, then call one direction positive, e.g. upwards, and stick to it.

12. Pace yourself. Don't go too quickly, as you will make silly mistakes. If you go too slowly, you don't finish. (You might be able to work out how long you have for each mark.) Leave yourself enough time at the end to check your answers.

13. When you do check, don't just passively look at your answers. You have to effectively do the questions again. Cover up what you have written and then compare what you have worked out a second time. Do not assume your first answer was wrong.

14. Don't worry.

15. Be happy.

16. But be prepared.

index

A
a.c. generator 66
acceleration 7
acceleration due to gravity 10
accommodation, eye 43
air resistance 10
alpha decay 81
alpha radiation 82
ampere 46
amplifier, current 75
amplitude 24, 27, 30
AND gate 77
angle, critical 37
angle, incidence 34, 36
angle, reflection 34
angle, refraction 35–36
anvil (ear) 30
apparent depth 36
Archimedes' principle 19
atmospheric pressure 19
atomic number 80
atomic structure 80–81
atoms 80, 81
average speed 6

B
bar magnets 57–58
base, transistor 75–76
batteries 52
becquerel 82
beta decay 81
beta radiation 82–83
bias, diodes 72
bicycle dynamo 66
big bang 95
blue shift 95
boiling point 91–92
Brownian motion 88

C
capacitors 73
carbon dioxide 12, 91
cells, electrical 47–48
centre of gravity 18
centre of mass 18
centre, optical 39
centrifugal forces 13
centripetal forces 13
charge, electronic 46–47
charge, static 46
charges, relative 80
ciliary muscles (eye) 43
circuit, parallel 47–48
circuit, series 47–48
circuits, electric 46–47
circular motion 13
cochlea (ear) 30
coil, primary 67
coil, secondary 67
collector, transistor 75
collisions 14–17
commutator 61
compass 56
compression, sound 29
concave lenses 38–39, 43
conduction 89
conductors, electrical 46
conductors, heat 89
conservation of energy 11
conservation of momentum 14
constant acceleration 8
constellations 95
constructive interference 27
convection 90–91
convection currents 90–91
convex lens ray diagrams 39–41
convex lenses 38–43
core, iron 59, 67
cornea (eye) 43
coulomb 46
crest (waves) 24, 27
critical angle 37
current, electric 46
currents, convection 90–91

D
d.c. motor 61
day 96
decay, radioactive 81–82
delocalised electrons 89
density 19
depth, apparent 36
depth, real 36
demagnetising a magnet 57
destructive interference 27
detectors, radiation 82
diffraction 26
diffuse reflection 35
diffusion 88
digital electronics 76–78
diode, *V–I* graph 49
diodes 72–73, 76
direct current motor 61
direction 7
displacement 6, 7
displacement–time graphs 7
distance 6
domains 56
double insulation 54
dynamo 64–66
dynamo effect 64

E
ear 30
Earth 95–96
echoes 29
efficiency 12
elastic collisions 16–17
elastic limit 18
electric circuits 46–47
electric current 46
electrical power 52
electrical resistance 48–51
electricity, mains 53–54
electricity, static 46
electromagnetic spectrum 27–28
electromagnetic waves 27
electromagnets 59
electronic charge 46–47
electronics, digital 76–78
electrons 46, 80
emitter, transistor 75
energy 12, 15–17, 24, 47, 53, 68, 84, 88–92, 98
energy, fuels 12
energy, nuclear 12, 84
energy, renewable sources of 12
energy, thermal 12, 89–92
energy, waves 24
environment 12
equilibrium 17, 18, 24
equilibrium position 24
explosions 14–15
eye 43
eye, accommodation 43

F
Faraday's Law 64
field lines 57
fields, electromagnetic 59
fields, magnetic 57
final velocity 7
finite fuels 12
Fleming's Left-hand Rule 60
Fleming's Right-hand Rule 64
fluids 19
focal length 39
focus 38, 39
forces 11, 13, 14, 17–19
forces, centrifugal 13
forces, centripetal 13
forces, friction 18
forces, upthrust 19
forward bias 72
fossil fuels 12
frequency 25–27, 30
frequency, natural 30
friction 18
fuels 12

G
galaxies 94
galvanometer 61, 67
galvanometer, moving-coil 61

gamma emission 81
gamma radiation 83
gases 89
gates, logic 77–78
generator 64
global warming 12, 91
gold-foil experiment 80
graphs, displacement–time 7
gravitational field strength 10
gravitational potential energy 11
gravity 96
greenhouse effect 12, 91
greenhouse gases 12, 91

H

half-life 82
hammer (ear) 30
heat 12, 89–92
high-grade energy 12
Hooke's Law 18
household electrical cost 53

I

image distance 42
image in a plane mirror 34
images, lateral inversion 34
images, real 34
images, virtual 34
impulse 14
incus (ear) 30
induced current 64
induced voltage 64
induction, magnetic 57
inelastic collisions 15
inertia 13
initial velocity 8
input, logical 76
insulation, double 54
insulation, household 89
insulators, electrical 46
insulators, heat 89
interference, constructive 27
interference, destructive 27
internal resistance 52
inverse-square law 83
inverter, logic gate 77
ions 80
iron core 59, 67
isotopes 81

J

joule 11, 52, 89

K

kilowatt-hour 53
kinematics 6–9
kinetic energy 11, 15, 16, 17, 89
kinetic theory 88–89
Kirchhoff's First Law 48

L

lateral inversion 34
LDRs 74
LEDs 73
Left-hand Rule 60
lenses 38–43
lenses, concave 38–39, 43
lenses, convex 38–43
lenses, eye 43
Lenz's Law 65
light-dependent resistors 74
light-dependent switch 75–76
light-emitting diodes 73
light year 33
light, point source 33
light, rectilinear propagation 33
light, reflection 34–35
light, refraction 35–36
light, visible 27, 28
linear magnification 42
liquids 89
logic 76–78
logic gates 77–78
logic gates, truth tables 77
longitudinal waves 24, 28, 29
long-sightedness 43
loudness 30
low-grade energy 12

M

magnetic effect of a current 58–59
magnetic fields 57–58
magnetically hard 56
magnetic induction 57
magnetic north 56
magnetic poles 56
magnetic resonance imaging (MRI) 59
magnetic south 56
magnetically soft 56, 57
magnetised material 56, 57
magnets 56–58
magnets, bar 57–58
magnets, compass 56, 57
magnets, demagnetisation 57
magnets, field lines 57
magnification, linear 42
magnitude 7
mains electricity 53–54
malleus (ear) 30
mass 11, 13, 14, 80
mass number 81
mass, centre of 18
mass, inertia 13
mechanics 6–19
medium 29, 35
melting point 91
microwaves 27, 28
mirages 38
moments 17
momentum 14–17
momentum, collisions 14–17
momentum, elastic collisions 16–17
momentum, explosions 14–15
momentum, impulse 14
momentum, inelastic collisions 15
moon 95
motion, circular 13
motor 60–61
motor effect 60–61
moving-coil galvanometer 61
MRI 59
musical instruments, timbre 30

N

NAND gate 78
natural frequency 30
neutral equilibrium 18
neutral point 58
neutron star 94
neutrons 80
newton 11
Newton's First Law 13
Newton's Second Law 13
Newton's Third Law 18
NOR gate 78
normal (optics) 35
normal (waves) 26
NOT gate 77
N-pole 56
nuclear energy 84–85
nuclear fission 84
nuclear power station 85
nuclear reactor 85
nucleon 80

O

object distance 42
ohm 48
ohmic resistors 49
optical centre 39
OR gate 77
orbit 95–97
oscillations 24–25
output, logical 76

P

P waves 24
parallel circuit 47–48
parallel resistance formula 51
pascal 19
penumbra 33
phase, in phase 24, 27
phase, out of phase 24, 27
pinhole camera 34
pinna (ear) 30
pitch 30
pivot 17
plane mirror, image in 34
plane mirror, reflection 25
plug, wiring 53–54
p–n junctions 72
point source, light 33
polarisation 28
potential difference 47
potential divider 70–72
potential divider equation 72
potential energy 11
potentiometer 70–72
power, electrical 52
power, lenses 42
power, mechanical 12
power, solar 12
prenatal scanning 29
pressure 19

pressure, atmospheric 19
pressure, in fluids 19
primary coil 67
principal axis 38, 39, 40
principal focus 38–42
principle, conservation of
energy 11
momentum 14
projectiles 10
protons 80
pupil (eye) 43

R

radiation detectors 82
radiation, alpha 82
radiation, beta 82–83
radiation, gamma 83
radiation, heat 91
radiation, nuclear 82–83
radiators 90
radio waves 28
radioactive decay 81–84
radioactive decay, alpha 81
radioactive decay, beta 81
radioactivity 82
radioisotopes 84
radioisotopes, uses of 84
rarefaction, sound 29
ray 25
ray diagrams, convex lenses 39–40
real depth 36
real images 34
rectifiers 72
rectilinear propagation 33
red giant 94
red shift 95
reed relay 74–75
reed switch 74
reflection 34–35
reflection, diffuse 35
reflection, echoes 29
reflection, plane mirror 25
refraction 35
refraction in semicircular block 37
refraction, light 35–36
refractive index 35
renewable energy sources 12
renewable fuels 12
resistance formulae, derivation 51
resistance, air 10
resistance, electrical 48
resistance, internal 52
resistance, parallel 51
resistance, series 51
resistor, *V–I* graph 49
resistors 49, 50, 52
resistors, LDRs 74
resistors, non-ohmic 50
resistors, ohmic 49
resistors, variable 70
resonance 30
reverse-bias 72
rheostat 70
Right-hand Grip Rule 58
Right-hand Rule 64
ripple tank 25–26

S

S waves 24
satellites 97
scalar 7
secondary coil 67
seismology 24
seismology, P waves 24
seismology, S waves 24
semiconductors 72
semiconductors, diodes 72
series circuits 47–48
series resistance formula 51
shadows 33
shadows, penumbra 33
shadows, umbra 33
short-sightedness 43
SI units appendix a
Slinky spring 24
slip rings 66
soft magnetic materials 56, 57
solar power 12
solar system 95–96
solenoid 59
solids 88
sonar 29
sound 29–30
sound, compression 29
sound, ear 30
sound, echoes 29
sound, loudness 30
sound, pitch 30
sound, rarefaction 29
sound, resonance 30
sound, sonar 29
sound, speed of 29
sound, timbre 30
spectrum, electromagnetic 27–28
speed 6
speed of sound 29
S-pole 56
springs, elastic limit 18
springs, Hooke's Law 18
springs, Slinky 24, 29
stable equilibrium 18
stapes (ear) 30
stars 94
static electricity 46
stirrup (ear) 30
Sun 95–96
supernova 94
suvat equations 7–8
systems, analogue 76
systems, digital 76
systems, electrical 76
systems, electronic 76

T

Thermos flask 91
timbre 30
time 7, 8
time period 25
total internal reflection 37–38
transducers 76
transformer equations 67–68
transformers 66–68
transistors 75–76
transverse waves 24, 27
trough 24
truth tables, logic gates 77
turning effect of a force 17

U

ultrasound 29
ultrasound, prenatal scanning 29
umbra 33
Universe 94
unstable equilibrium 18
upthrust 19
U-value 89

V

variable resistors 70
vector 7
velocity 7
vertical and horizontal motion 10
V–I graphs, diode 49
V–I graphs, lamp 49
V–I graphs, resistor 49
virtual images 34
volt 47
voltage, potential difference 47

W

watt 12, 52
wave equation 25, 29
waveform 30
wavefronts 25, 26
wavelength 24–29
waves, amplitude 24, 27, 30
waves, crest 24, 27
waves, diffraction 26
waves, electromagnetic 27–28
waves, equilibrium position 24
waves, frequency 25–27, 30
waves, interference 27
waves, longitudinal 24, 28, 29
waves, oscillations 24–25
waves, P 24
waves, phase 24, 27
waves, polarisation 28
waves, ray 25
waves, reflection 25
waves, refraction 26
waves, S 24
waves, Slinky spring model 24, 29
waves, sound 29
waves, time period 25
waves, transverse 24, 27
waves, trough 24
weight 13
white dwarf 94
work, mechanical 12

X

X-rays 27–28

Y

year 96